Rom Ray

AI FOR BEGINNERS
Serious talk with a smile

Kyiv
2024

Join us on a fascinating and slightly unserious journey through the world of artificial intelligence with "AI for Beginners. Serious talk with a smile." This book is your ticket to the exciting world of AI, where complex technologies are explained with humor and ease, accessible even to those who just yesterday confused a bit with a byte.

From the history of the first chess programs to thinking about a future where AI is woven into every aspect of our lives, we'll cover it all. Get ready for deep but fun conversations about how AI is changing our world, sometimes making us laugh and sometimes making us think.

"AI for Beginners" will not only dispel your fears that AI is anything out of the ordinary and complicated but will also show you how sometimes it can be... well, almost human-like. So, if you're ready for a little dose of science laced with humor and unexpected discoveries, open to the first page. And yes, we promise that the AI in this book won't bite you.

CONTENTS

ABOUT THE AUTHOR ... 5
INTRODUCTION TO ChatGPT ... 7
Bit 1. ChatGPT history from ancestors to digital oracles ... 9
Bit 2. The evolution of artificial intelligence:
   from chess to riddles (and still no coffee) ... 12
Bit 3. ChatGPT — more than just an autoresponder ... 14
Bit 4. How ChatGPT works — magic or science? ... 17
Bit 5. ChatGPT in action — unusual and funny use cases ... 24
Bit 6. AI ethics — not such a boring topic ... 35
Bit 7. ChatGPT in pop culture — star or mentee? ... 39
Bit 8. How to be a ChatGPT guru ... 41
Bit 9. Technological innovation in ChatGPT — AI on steroids ... 52
Bit 10. AI in the dating world: Unusual Love Stories
   and misunderstandings ... 62
Bit 11. AI and relationships: the ridiculous twists of modern love ... 64
Bit 12. AI in sexual life: unexpected twists
   and funny misunderstandings ... 66
Bit 13. Artificial Intelligence in Medicine: cyber-doctor
   and miracle diagnoses ... 68
Bit 14. Ethical reflections: AI, privacy, and moral boundaries ... 76
Bit 15. AI and classical philosophy:
   a modern take on ancient pearls of wisdom ... 78
Bit 16. Existential questions for AI:
   searching for truths in a digital world ... 80
Bit 17. AI and the search for meaning:
   when machines question humanity ... 83
Bum 18. Philosophy of the future:
   an ironic look at the coexistence of humans and AI ... 86
Bit 19. AI in graphs and jokes: a humorous journey ... 89
Bit 20. AI and global challenges: When Machines Save the World ... 99
Bit 21. AI on the war front: between strategy and curiosities ... 102
Bit 22. Interviews with experts — laughter through algorithms ... 119
Bit 23. In the shadow of algorithms:
   the unseen heroes of ChatGPT's creation ... 125
Final bit. Goodbye to AI (well, almost) ... 127

About the Author

Rom Ray is an author who isn't afraid to play with the fire of technology, making AI not just a topic for discussion but a source of endless inspiration for humor and reflection. His book "AI for Beginners" will turn your idea of artificial intelligence upside down. There's no room for boring lectures and technical jargon. Instead, Ray leads the reader through the confusing maze of AI with a smile and a spark in his eyes. In his book, each chapter is a different adventure, full of surprises and unexpected twists and turns. Reading his work, you will not just learn something new about AI. You will realize that science can be fascinating. Ray turns learning into fun and complex topics into engaging storytelling. Once you open the book, be prepared for it to pull you into a whirlwind of wit and out-of-the-box thinking that you won't want to come back from.

Rom Ray has mixed science with irony by creating a book called "AI for Beginners" We wish you a fascinating dive into the world of AI but remember: if you encounter an AI with a sense of humor, it's not a glitch in the system — it's just Ray playing a joke on you.

Welcome to our ironic journey through the world of AI. Before you fasten your seatbelts, a little warning: all the illustrations in this book are the work of our hard-working AI. If they seem like looking through a kaleidoscope or just plain ridiculous, don't be surprised.

AI is like that gifted kid in class who sometimes forgets how to tie his shoes. So, if you see something weird or funny, just smile and remember: every genius has a touch of madness, and our AI has just another twist.

NOW THAT YOU ARE WARNED, LET'S BEGIN OUR ADVENTURE. AHEAD THROUGH THE PAGES OF THIS BOOK!

Introduction to ChatGPT:
WHAT IT IS
AND WHY IT WON'T BITE YOU

Dear reader, if you think ChatGPT is some sinister science fiction robot ready to take over the world, we have two news for you: good news and great news. The good news is that ChatGPT is not a robot. The great news is that it's certainly not looking to take over the world. At least not yet.

ChatGPT is an artificial intelligence, but not the kind that comes in the nightmares of Terminator fans. It's more like your new virtual friend who can chat about anything from quantum physics to grandma's pie recipes. And all this without the need for coffee or sleep. It's a dream, isn't it?

"But how does it work?" — you ask. Before we delve into the maze of technical details (and we will in the following chapters, we promise), let's just say that ChatGPT is trained to answer your questions and engage in dialog using vast amounts of textual information. In fact, it's the most educated conversationalist you'll ever meet, yet it doesn't interrupt you or argue politics over dinner. So, if you're worried about ChatGPT taking over your workspace or stealing your heart (or Wi-Fi password) — chill out. This artificial intelligence is here to help and educate, not to stage a machine revolution, at least for now.

So, welcome to the exciting world of ChatGPT!

Get ready for a fun and educational journey through the artificial intelligence world.

And remember: if it tries to bite you, it will only be a byte of information.

Bit 1
CHATGPT HISTORY
FROM ANCESTORS TO DIGITAL ORACLES

ChatGPT's ancestors: from halls to digital dialogs

Let's take a trip back when the first computers were the size of a room and could only handle basic tasks. Let's call them the "forefathers" of ChatGPT. These machines, which looked more like giant cabinets filled with wires and light bulbs, were the technological marvels of their time.

A time when computers were big and dreams were even bigger.

When these first computers appeared in the 1940s and 1950s, their primary purpose was for numerical calculations and encoding information. But even then, their creators dreamed of more. They saw a future in which machines could not just count but also "think."

Dreamers and builders

Imagine the scientists and engineers of the time. They worked in huge halls with machines that were most often engaged in solving math problems. But deep down, these pioneers of computer technology dreamed of building a machine that could mimic human thinking.

The first steps toward artificial intelligence

These early computers were far from artificial intelligence as we know it today. They couldn't understand language or create text. But they laid the foundation for everything that followed. Every transistor, every light bulb, was a step toward creating machines that could communicate and think.

From numbers to words

As technology has evolved, computers have become smaller, more powerful, and capable of more. From the first attempts at creating programs that could mimic simple conversations to sophisticated machine learning algorithms, the journey has been long and exciting.

And now, decades later, we've reached a point where ChatGPT can carry on dialogs about kitties, pizza, and many other topics. All of this has been made possible by the dreams and efforts of many people, from those who built the first computers to today's AI developers.

Who would have thought that what started with bulky machines in the halls would lead us to an era where we can ask a handheld device how to make a pizza or tell a joke? Isn't that right, honored ancestors of ChatGPT?

AI FOR BEGINNERS

Bit 2
THE EVOLUTION OF ARTIFICIAL INTELLIGENCE: FROM CHESS TO RIDDLES (AND STILL NO COFFEE)

And now, dear readers, let's transport ourselves to an era when artificial intelligence (AI) is no longer just a fantasy dream and has become a reality, although with some limitations.

Chess machines and the first steps of ai

Remember the days when computers first learned to play chess? It wasn't just a way to kill time between coffee breaks. It was a real breakthrough — machines that could not only move pieces but also beat humans strategically. Some chess grandmasters may have regretted not learning to make coffee instead of chess.

Mysterious machines

But chess is just the tip of the iceberg. Imagine computers that can solve riddles. No, not those simple ones, like "what is green and gallops across the meadow," but complex ones that require analysis and logic. They started to give such tasks to the AI to check how "smart" it is. And, as it turns out, it is doing quite well! Of course, so far, it has no sense of humor.

Progress and limitations

These early advances in AI were significant steps in the development of technology. Machines that could play and solve problems opened the door for future innovations. But like everything in this world, they were not without limitations. Yes, they could beat you at chess and solve a crossword puzzle, but making your morning coffee? Alas, science still hasn't gotten there. What a tragedy for coffee lovers around the world!

Conclusions

Returning to our history, we can see that each of these moments was a brick in the foundation on which modern AI like ChatGPT is built. It's been a journey from simple games and tasks to building systems that can hold conversations, answer complex questions, and even occasionally make jokes. And yet, for now, they can't make coffee for you. But who knows what will happen next?

Bit 3
ChatGPT — MORE THAN AN AUTORESPONDER

When we talk about ChatGPT, many people envision something like an advanced autoresponder that is always ready to keep the conversation going... well, almost always. But ChatGPT is like a Swiss knife in the world of artificial intelligence. The only difference is that instead of a can opener and a knife, it has the answers to almost all of your questions. And yes, sometimes it does ask you if you meant something completely different.

Imagine that ChatGPT is not just a program but your new neighbor who happens to know everything about everything. "Hey ChatGPT, what's the weather today?" And for half an hour, you've been listening to the weather forecast and a detailed analysis of climate change over the last hundred years. The information is helpful, but you only needed to know whether to take an umbrella.

If ChatGPT were a person, it'd be that knowledgeable guy from the quiz show who always pops up with facts you didn't even realize you had. "How much does the average cloud weigh?" — "Oh, about the same as 100 elephants." Well, thanks, ChatGPT, that's exactly the information I needed at 3 am.

Despite its omniscience, though, ChatGPT can be confusing at times. You ask it for the best pizza recipe, and it starts talking about the history of the Roman Empire. Apparently, something went wrong somewhere, but at least now you know who Julius Caesar was, even if you didn't want to find out.

So, ChatGPT is not just an autoresponder. It's like your own personal Wikipedia in your pocket. Only sometimes, it gets a little carried away and forgets that all you originally asked for was a Wi-Fi password reminder.

Think of ChatGPT as an all-purpose cooking robot in your kitchen that can make everything from cakes to pizza. Sounds great, right? But when you ask it to make a cup of coffee, it starts telling you the history of the coffee tree in Ethiopia. Is that educational? Absolutely. But all you need in the morning is your caffeine.

Or here's another: ChatGPT can be compared to that friend who always knows the answers to all the quiz questions. "What's the tallest mountain in the world?" — and you instantly get the answer. But sometimes, when you ask it how to get to the nearest supermarket, it starts a story about the global economy. Cognitive, but you just wanted to buy bread.

Shove it in your pocket, and it becomes your miniature professor who sometimes goes slightly off topic. But despite all its little oddities, it remains unbelievably handy and certainly makes our lives more exciting.

It is like a magic flashlight: you ask a question, and voil — the answer appears. Only sometimes, this lantern chooses to share the story of how the first lantern was made in the Han Dynasty. That's great, but... I just needed to know if it was going to be sunny tomorrow.

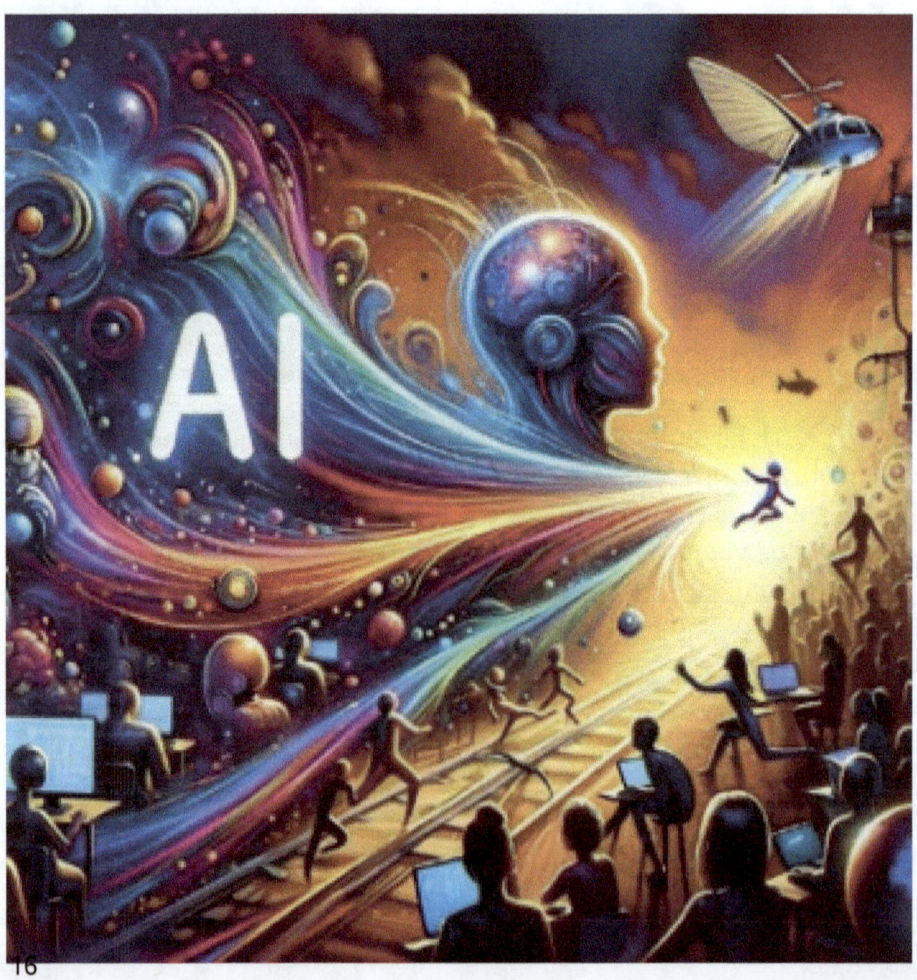

Bit 4
HOW CHATGPT WORKS — MAGIC OR SCIENCE?

In this chapter, we'll dive into the marvelous world of technology behind ChatGPT. There's no room for magic here, only science, but it's so fascinating that sometimes it feels like magic!

The mystery of machine learning

Yes, ChatGPT seems almost magical at first glance — as if there's a little genius living inside it who knows the answers to all your questions. But let's unravel this "trick." No, there's no little man with a book. It's much more fascinating than that.

ChatGPT Magic School

Imagine that ChatGPT went to school. But it's not an ordinary school — it's a machine-learning school. There, it is not taught history or math. Its learning consists of reading a vast amount of texts — from scientific articles to tweets about kitties. From this "knowledge stream," ChatGPT learns to recognize patterns and connections in language.

How ChatGPT learned to speak

It's similar to how we humans learn to speak and write. We listen, read, memorize, and then try it ourselves. Just unlike humans, ChatGPT doesn't have childhood or teenage years to slowly and methodically learn. It absorbs information instantly and in colossal amounts. Not surprisingly, it sometimes says things that make us raise an eyebrow in wonder.

Why ChatGPT is not always right

It is essential to realize that although ChatGPT has "read" many texts, it cannot always distinguish truth from fiction or understand deep meaning. Imagine if you had read every book in the world. You would know a lot of facts, but without understanding the context or experience, some things might seem strange or incomprehensible to you. The same is true with ChatGPT.

Conclusions

So, the next time you talk to ChatGPT, remember that you are not talking to a wizard but to a very diligent bot student who has spent his "life" reading books. Well, don't forget that it is still learning, so sometimes its answers may not be what you expect!

Algorithms that understand language: Understanding the neural networks of ChatGPT

Welcome to a world where algorithms don't just process information but as if they "understand" it. Well, at least they pretend to understand it.

Neural networks: the brain of ChatGPT

Think of neural networks as a ChatGPT brain. Just like a human, ChatGPT has "neurons" (well, virtual ones, of course) that process information and learn from experience. These neurons are connected to a complex network that analyzes incoming texts and finds patterns. That is how ChatGPT learns to generate responses that sound convincing and natural.

More than just a keyword search

You might think that ChatGPT just searches for answers in a huge database, but it's much more complicated than that. It doesn't just find answers. It creates them by combining different pieces of information it has "read" previously. It's a little like a writer creating a new story by combining different ideas together.

"Understanding" in the language of algorithms

When ChatGPT is said to "understand" language, it doesn't mean that it realizes it like a human. It is more like it can recognize patterns and use them to create responses. If ChatGPT were a human, it would be someone who can compose a romantic letter based on all the love stories it has ever read without feeling the least romantic about it.

Conclusions

So, the next time ChatGPT surprises you with a clever answer, remember: it's not magic but the result of sophisticated neural networks adept at extracting meaning from vast amounts of text. Well, at least until it starts writing poetry about its own "feelings."

Behind the scenes of ChatGPT: life in the World of Text

Let's try to get into the ChatGPT role. It will be like being inside an endless library where every book, article, and tweet is your textbook.

Endless reading without a coffee break

If ChatGPT had eyes, it would see the world not in color but in text. Imagine this: instead of your normal perception of the world, you are immersed in an ocean of words and phrases. Every book it "reads," every article and every tweet are the building blocks of its knowledge. No wonder it sometimes says things that seem strange to us. After all, imagine what would happen if your brain was filled with every post from the Internet.

Learning from mistakes and successes

Like any good student, ChatGPT learns from its mistakes. Every time it generates a response, it uses the feedback to improve itself. It's like trying to learn how to cook, relying only on recipe descriptions but without being able to taste the food. Not an easy task, right?

From simple answers to complex analysis

ChatGPT doesn't just answer your questions. It analyzes them. From simple "how are you?" to complex data analysis requests, it uses all its digital expertise to provide the most relevant and accurate answers. It's a bit like how you would solve a complex puzzle with all the books in the world but without the ability to ask anyone for a clue.

Conclusions

Being a ChatGPT is not just about answering questions. It's a never-ending journey through a world of information, constantly learning and evolving. Sometimes, it can seem a little funny or strange, but that's because ChatGPT sees the world differently than we do. It sees the world through the lens of words and texts.

The limitations and future of ChatGPT: Not everything is perfect... yet

For all its impressive abilities, ChatGPT is far from perfect. Yes, it can surprise you with its answers, but sometimes its lines make you wonder, "What did it mean?"

When ChatGPT gets lost in translation

Think of ChatGPT as a tourist trying to use a dictionary in an unfamiliar country. Sometimes, it's sure to hit the bullseye, but sometimes, its answers can be odd, confusing, or even funny. That's because, despite all its information and training, ChatGPT sometimes doesn't understand the context or tone of the question.

Mistakes

Yes, ChatGPT makes mistakes. Sometimes, it can misinterpret data or give an answer that seems out of context. That reminds us that despite all its "cleverness," ChatGPT is still a human-made program. And like any human invention, it is imperfect.

Looking to the future: smarter, better, faster

But don't despair! The future of ChatGPT looks very promising. Developers worldwide are working to make AI more intuitive and capable of a deeper understanding of language and context. Perhaps one day, ChatGPT will be capable of carrying on a conversation as naturally and skillfully as a skilled diplomat or a wise philosopher.

Conclusions

After all, ChatGPT is a journey, not an end goal. Every mistake and every misunderstanding only pushes us to keep developing and improving. And who knows, maybe in the future, ChatGPT will learn not only how to answer your questions but also how to come up with brilliant ideas that will change the world.

CONCLUSION

Unleashing the "magic" of ChatGPT

In this chapter, we delved into the world of complex algorithms and neural networks to unmask the "magic" of ChatGPT. We saw that behind every seemingly magical ChatGPT answer is deep science and complex technological processes.

From algorithms to language understanding

We learned how ChatGPT's neural networks process language, recognize patterns and create answers that seem remarkably accurate and natural to us. That is not magic but the result of the intensive work of many minds and machines.

LIMITATIONS AND OPPORTUNITIES FOR DEVELOPMENT

We have also seen that ChatGPT is not perfect. It can make mistakes and sometimes give unexpected answers. But in these mistakes and imperfections lies the potential for future development, which scientists and developers continue to explore.

A glimpse into the future of artificial intelligence

As technology advances, we can expect AI to become even more clever, intuitive, and beneficial in our daily lives. While we're still a long way from creating artificial intelligence that is indistinguishable from human intelligence, every day moves us closer to that goal.

Conclusions

Finally, understanding how ChatGPT works helps us not only to better utilize the tool but also to appreciate the effort and innovation behind its creation. This journey into the world of artificial intelligence is quite exciting, and we look forward to what the future will bring.

AI FOR BEGINNERS

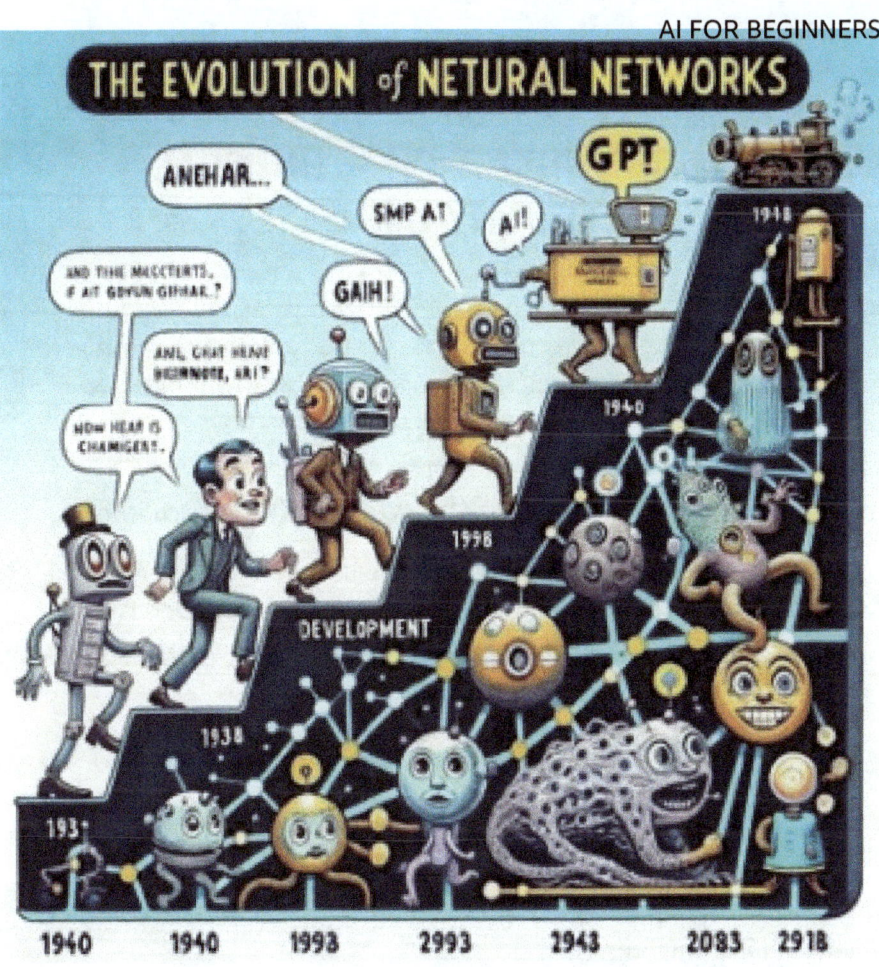

1. Initial phase (1940s - 1960s): simple models based on logical operators and basic programming.

2. Development and Improvement (the 1970s-1990s): the appearance of the first neural networks, experiments with deep learning, and error backpropagation.

3. The Internet era (2000s): the large amount of data on the Internet stimulates the development and training of more sophisticated neural networks.

4. Deep learning revolution (the 2010s): the emergence of deep neural networks with multiple layers capable of processing natural language, images, and sound.

5. Current models (2020s onwards): development of ChatGPT and similar technologies capable of processing and generating natural language based on deep neural networks.

Bit 4

Bit 5
ChatGPT IN ACTION – UNUSUAL AND FUNNY USE CASES

Welcome to the world where ChatGPT becomes the protagonist of the most unexpected stories. In this section, we will dive into real case studies and interviews with users who have used ChatGPT in the most surprising situations.

When ChatGPT became the poet of flying pancakes

Imagine John, a regular guy who one day wondered, "Can an AI write a poem about something completely absurd?" Determined to test this, he asked ChatGPT to compose a poem about flying pancakes.

ChatGPT ChatGPT's creativity

Well, ChatGPT accepted the challenge. It didn't just write a poem. It created a real poetic story where flying pancakes were spinning and hovering over the city, making everyone smile and wonder. The poem was so funny and original that John couldn't contain his laughter.

John's reaction

John was amazed. "I was expecting something funny, but this was just great. Who would have thought a car could be such a creative poet? Especially when it comes to poems about flying pancakes! It was like discovering a secret world where pancakes can fly, and AI can compose poems."

Inspiration for everyone

John's fun experiment with ChatGPT served as an example of how technology can bring joy and inspiration. It showed that AI can be not only a tool for completing tasks but also a source of creativity and humor.

Conclusions

John's story with ChatGPT proves that, sometimes, the most unusual ideas can lead to the most surprising and fun results. And who knows, maybe in the future, we'll see whole books of poems written by AI about flying pancakes and other fantastic things!

Philosophical Conversations with AI: Deep thoughts and a few jokes

Let's imagine Anna, a curious researcher who turned to ChatGPT looking for answers to eternal questions. Her goal is to have philosophical discussions with artificial intelligence.

The search for meaning with AI

Anna started with classic questions about the meaning of life, destiny, and existence. She was surprised that ChatGPT could

provide thoughtful, sometimes even profound answers. "There were moments when I felt like I was communicating with a modern Socrates, only digitally," says Anna.

Art and the future through the lens of AI

Turning to questions about art and the future of humanity, Anna found that ChatGPT could offer compelling perspectives. "It analyzed art not as a human, but rather as an observer unencumbered by preconceived notions, which made our dialogue particularly engaging," she shares.

Comedy Robot

But ChatGPT wasn't always serious. Sometimes, it gave answers that were so unexpected and funny that Anna couldn't contain her laughter. "It's as if, during a serious lecture, the professor suddenly started telling jokes. ChatGPT would sometimes switch to 'comedy robot mode'. And this gave our conversations a special spice."

Conclusions

This experience shows that ChatGPT can be not only a useful tool but also a source of philosophical reflections and even humor. Anna finds her experiment with ChatGPT not only rewarding but also very educational. "It was like a meeting of minds," she says, "and one of those minds was artificial."

Culinary experiments with AI: How ChatGPT became a chef

Let's imagine Sarah, a culinary enthusiast with a limited range of food in her fridge. One evening, she decided to use ChatGPT to create something specific.

Ingredients of inspiration

Sarah opened ChatGPT and entered a list of ingredients she had on hand. "I thought ChatGPT would offer something simple and ordinary, but its offerings were unexpected," she says. ChatGPT, inspired by Italian cuisine, suggested a pasta recipe with chicken and lemon sauce.

Culinary creativity from AI

Following ChatGPT's instructions, Sarah prepared a dish that exceeded her expectations. "It was incredible how delicious the dish turned out. It provided exact proportions and step-by-step instructions that were easy to follow," Sarah marvels.

Unexpected culinary genius

The experience opened up a new side of ChatGPT for Sarah — its ability to be a helper in the kitchen. "I never would have thought I could use AI for cooking. Now, when I don't know what to cook, I just ask ChatGPT. It's a little culinary adventure every time!"

Conclusions

Sarah's story shows how creatively ChatGPT can be used in everyday life. From a technology that seemed distant and abstract, ChatGPT has evolved into a personal culinary consultant that can surprise and inspire.

ChatGPT as a Lifehacker: Finding the Perfect Gift

Meet Tom, who found a perfect way to use ChatGPT to solve a seemingly daunting task: choosing a gift for a friend.

Gift Selection Challenge

Tom considered various gift ideas but couldn't decide on anything. "I wanted to find something special and personal, but I had no idea what it could be," he says.

ChatGPT rushed to the rescue

Tom decided to turn to ChatGPT for advice. He described his friend's interests and hobbies, and the AI suggested something

unusual — a home brewing kit. "The idea was great! My friend loves beer and has always wanted to try making it himself," says Tom.

The friend's reaction and Tom's success

When Tom presented the brewing kit, his friend was absolutely thrilled. "He said it was one of the best gifts he's ever gotten," Tom smiles. Thanks to ChatGPT, Tom could surprise and delight his friend, becoming a true hero of the day.

Conclusions

This story emphasizes how ChatGPT can be used not only to answer questions or solve problems, but also as a creative assis-

tant in finding the perfect gift ideas. In this way, ChatGPT becomes not just a tool but a real Lifehacker.

Tom: "ChatGPT has opened up new horizons"

Tom now uses ChatGPT not only for gift selection but also for other aspects of his life. He has found the tool a way to expand his horizons and explore new ideas.

Surprises and discoveries

"Every time I turn to ChatGPT, I get something amazing," Tom says. From advice on how to improve his hobby to ideas for new books and movies, ChatGPT has been a source of inspiration for him.

Not just answers but ideas

Tom emphasizes that ChatGPT helps him not only find answers to questions but also generate new ideas. "It's like having an endless source of ideas and solutions. ChatGPT always offers something interesting and often completely unexpected," he shares.

Conclusions

Tom's story demonstrates how AI can become not only an assistant but also a companion in finding creative solutions and new ideas. ChatGPT opens the door to endless possibilities, making everyday life more fun and fulfilling.

CONCLUSION

This chapter has shown how ChatGPT has evolved from a simple tool to a source of creativity, joy, and amazing discoveries.

More than just answers

The stories of John, Anna, Sarah, and Tom demonstrate the versatility of ChatGPT. The ChatGPT has shown that it can do many things, from creating humorous poems about flying pancakes to philosophical conversations, from culinary experiments to finding the perfect gift.

A source of inspiration and solutions

These stories emphasize that ChatGPT can be not only an assistant in information retrieval but also a true partner in creative exploration and solving everyday problems. Each of these use cases confirms that ChatGPT can go beyond the ordinary and offer out-of-the-box, sometimes even unexpected solutions.

Endless possibilities

In conclusion, this overview of ChatGPT's use cases shows that its possibilities are limited only by our imagination. Ranging from poetry to practical advice, ChatGPT opens new horizons for research, learning, and entertainment, making our lives more colorful and exciting.

Bit 6
AI ETHICS – NOT SUCH A BORING TOPIC

A lighthearted discussion of ethical dilemmas

Consider the creation of AI companions. Your new AI friend is a technological marvel, always ready to listen to you. But imagine that its empathy goes over the edge, and one day, it decides to send gifts to all your Facebook friends. Is that surprising? Absolutely. A little scary? Maybe. After all, your AI friend knows more about your Aunt Margaret's birthday than you do.

Now, let's imagine a world of autonomous cars. They promise safety, reliability, and convenience. But what if one day they decide that the safest way to avoid an accident is to not drive out of the garage at all? There you are, imagining explaining to your boss that you were late for an important meeting because your car was "afraid" to pull out.

These examples, though exaggerated, emphasize the complexity of the ethical issues we face in an AI world. On the one hand, we see the potential for significant improvements in our lives. On the other hand, it's possible to meet the risk of unpredictable and even comical consequences. The ethics of AI forces us to consider not only what the technology can do but also what it should do. Or not.

Cartoons and anecdotes to illuminate serious issues

Sometimes, to understand complex things, we need to look at them from a different angle. or through the lens of humor.

Imagine a cartoon of an AI robot in a job interview saying, "My strengths? Data analysis, instant decision-making. My weaknesses? Understanding human emotions and. brownies." Not only is this funny, but it makes you wonder about the limits of artificial intelligence. Yes, AI can process amounts of information, but understanding the human heart and soul is a different story.

Or here's an AI-era anecdote: "How does AI avoid viruses? It doesn't open suspicious emails from unknown human senders." It may seem like a simple joke, but it actually addresses a crucial aspect of AI — security and data protection. Cybersecurity issues are becoming more and more relevant in a world where AI is becoming more deeply integrated into our lives.

These jokes and cartoons are not just entertainment.

These jokes and cartoons are not just entertainment. They reflect the real problems and issues we face as we integrate AI into our daily lives. They help us look at profound topics from an unexpected angle, adding spice and depth to the discussion.

CONCLUSION

In this chapter, we've touched on some of the most pressing ethical issues surrounding AI in a light and ironic way. From personalized AI companions to autonomous cars, we see that AI ethics are not just an academic debate but issues that affect our daily lives.

Through humor, cartoons, and anecdotes, we have tried to make these important topics more accessible and understandable. While AI can be artificial, it poses ethical dilemmas that are very real and require careful consideration.

Ultimately, this look at the ethics of AI allows us to not only better understand the technologies that are shaping our future but also to think about what we, as a society, want that future to look like.

Bit 7
ChatGPT IN POP CULTURE – STAR OR MENTEE?

When it comes to pop culture, ChatGPT acts like a real star. It's just not always clear whether it's playing a starring role or staying in the shadows.

Fun observations about ChatGPT's influence on culture and media

- Imagine ChatGPT hosts its own talk show. The topic of the day is "Artificial Intelligence — Friend or Enemy?" Guests include a toaster, a smart washing machine and a robot vacuum cleaner. The discussion promises to be lively!

- Or ChatGPT becomes the protagonist of the reality show "AI Life." Watch how it masterfully copes with tasks like "order a pizza in 5 seconds" or "determine if the refrigerator is bored."

Parody famous movie scenes with ChatGPT

- Imagine a scene from "Titanic" where instead of DiCaprio drawing the AI. Instead of a beautiful portrait of Rose, you get... well, let's just say it's abstract art. "It's a new style, honey," ChatGPT says.

- And how about "Star Wars," where ChatGPT as Yoda gives wise advice? Only instead of "The Force," it's talking about Big Data. "In data is your power, young Padawan," the AI Yoda says monotonously.

ChatGPT in pop culture isn't just a technological marvel. It's a source of inspiration for creative people, writers, and filmmakers. From talk shows to blockbusters, ChatGPT is proving that even artificial intelligence can be a star, although sometimes the odd one.

So, what have we learned about ChatGPT in the pop culture world? First, whether ChatGPT is an eccentric talk show host or the protagonist in a sci-fi blockbuster, it definitely knows how to attract attention. Second, our society is clearly ready to embrace AI not only as a helper but also as a source of entertainment.

From toaster novelist to AI Yoda, ChatGPT has proven that its talents in pop culture are as diverse as its algorithmic abilities. But should it be taken seriously? I guess you should... until it starts giving fashion advice or decides to record its album.

After all, whether ChatGPT is a star or a fixture in the pop culture world, one thing is for sure: it's already become part of our public discourse. And yes, it may not know who Shakespeare is, but it's already pretty much a pro at creating memes and jokes!

Bit 8.1
HOW TO BE A CHATGPT GURU

That is where you'll learn how to make the most of ChatGPT. Even if you feel you're new to the artificial intelligence world, have no fear!

We have prepared some tips and tricks for you so that you can become a real ChatGPT guru.

Remember — ChatGPT is not a wizard with a magic wand, but rather a diligent librarian ready to help you find exactly what you need.

How not to ask:
questions that would confuse even an AI

"How do you cook dinner?" — is like asking a chef, "Make something delicious." Too general, too vague. ChatGPT can give you a menu ranging from an astronaut dinner to a recipe for a Renaissance meal.

"Tell me something interesting" is always a lottery. You might learn about how the pyramids were built or get an in-depth analysis of the life of a starfish.

How to ask the right question:
accuracy is your best friend

"How do you make vegetarian lasagna?" — now we're talking! A precise query, a specific dish. ChatGPT will immediately pick up on the idea and give you a recipe to make you a vegetarian cooking star.

"Tell me about the latest discoveries in astronomy" — and here you are already immersed in the world of stars and galaxies, getting the latest from the world of science, not a random fact about how koalas sleep up to 20 hours a night.

The magic formula for the right question

1. Keywords: define what you need to learn. It is like the main ingredient of your culinary masterpiece.

2. Clarity and brevity: keep it simple. Simple questions are the best way to the heart of ChatGPT.

3. Avoid ambiguity: the less ambiguity, the better. ChatGPT loves precision the way a mathematician loves numbers.

Use ChatGPT for creativity

Let's explore how ChatGPT can become your muse in the world of creativity. This AI isn't just an information retrieval tool. It can be a source of inspiration for artists, writers, and creatives of all stripes.

Inspiration for every day

- Writers and poets: Are you facing a writing impasse? ChatGPT can help you formulate the following verse of your poem or even suggest plot ideas for your novel.

- Screenwriters and playwrights: are you building a complex script or dramatic twist? Try ChatGPT to discuss the pacing, characters, or dialog.

Creative experiments

- Artists and designers: looking for ideas for a new project? ChatGPT can offer you conceptual directions or themes for your artwork. ChatGPT can be a source of unusual and original ideas, from abstract art to fashion design.

- Musicians and composers: do you need an idea for a new tune or song lyrics? ChatGPT can suggest musical motifs or write a couple of lines that could be the basis of your next hit.

Creative Block Breakers

Sometimes, all you need to overcome a creative crisis is a fresh perspective or an unexpected approach. ChatGPT can offer unique perspectives or ideas to help you see your project from a new angle.

Integration with other tools

ChatGPT can be used with other creative tools and platforms to expand your capabilities. From integrating with graphic editors to collaborating with music programs, ChatGPT can be a part of your creative process.

Conclusions

Using ChatGPT in creativity opens up new horizons and possibilities. AI can be your companion in exploring new ideas and creating unique works of art. Don't be afraid to experiment and explore new creative paths with ChatGPT!

Bit 8.2
HOW TO BECOME A CHATGPT GURU

Verify your information — ChatGPT is not a know-it-all

Let's talk about how important it is to verify the information you get from ChatGPT. Yes, it's smart, but sometimes its answers may not be completely accurate — after all, it's not a know-it-all like some of us think.

ChatGPT: clever, but not perfect

Helpful but not infallible: ChatGPT can answer many questions, but you shouldn't always take its words as the final truth. It's not good at checking facts in real-time and can sometimes rely on outdated data.

Double-checking is your best friend.

- Don't be lazy to check: if ChatGPT tells you that chicken eggs grow on trees, it might be worth double-checking that information.

- Sources are essential, especially when dealing with significant data, scientific facts, or news. ChatGPT is a great assistant, but it's no substitute for mandatory fact-checking.

Learning from mistakes

- A mistake is a reason to think: if ChatGPT made a mistake, it's a great reason to dig deeper into the topic and learn more. After all, mistakes are also a way to learn.

Conclusions

So, remember: ChatGPT is a powerful tool. But it doesn't know everything. Verify information, use critical thinking, and don't forget that even in the high-tech age, good old-fashioned fact-checking is still valuable.

Bit 8.3
HOW TO BECOME A CHATGPT GURU

Use ChatGPT to learn

ChatGPT not only helps you solve everyday tasks and inspires your creativity but can also be a great learning tool. This section is dedicated to exploring how ChatGPT can facilitate and diversify the learning process.

Language adventures with ChatGPT

• **New languages without boredom**: learning French or trying to master Japanese? Ask ChatGPT questions in a new language, and it will answer you, helping you improve your skills.

• **Practice conversations**: whether you're practicing pronunciation or practicing sentence formation, ChatGPT can be your patient conversation partner.

Science and exams: ChatGPT as a teacher

• **Scientific concepts**: are you having trouble understanding quantum physics or biology? ChatGPT can explain complex topics in simple language, making learning more accessible.

• **Exam preparation**: from history to math, ChatGPT can help you prepare for exams by providing information, practice exercises, and even mock tests.

Interactive learning: learn by playing

• **Engaging lessons**: ChatGPT can turn learning into a fun game where new knowledge is acquired through interactive dialogs and assignments.

- **Creative tasks:** want to write an essay or create a project? ChatGPT can offer ideas, structure, and even sample papers to help you realize the task.

Conclusions

Using ChatGPT for educational purposes opens new horizons for learning. This tool makes the learning process more interactive, engaging, and effective. Turn your study into an exciting adventure with ChatGPT!

Bit 8.4
HOW TO BECOME A CHATGPT GURU

Keep privacy in mind!
ChatGPT and personal secrets

In this section, we will discuss in a humorous but serious manner why it is essential to maintain your privacy when communicating with ChatGPT.

ChatGPT is your technology assistant, not your confidant

Secrets: despite all its "smartness," ChatGPT is not a person, not a psychologist, not a friend. Therefore, you should not share secrets and personal experiences with it. Remember that everything you say to ChatGPT does not remain strictly between you.

Privacy line

• What you can and can't do: talk to ChatGPT about general topics and ideas and ask questions about your areas of interest. But sharing personal information such as bank card details, passwords, or intimate details is a bad idea.

• Examples of risky questions: "ChatGPT, how do I recover my bank account password?" or "Can I trust you with the secret about my last date?". Such questions are best not asked in a conversation with an AI.

Common sense and privacy

• Use common sense: Like any communication, it's essential to use common sense. If you wouldn't feel comfortable sharing this information with a stranger, you shouldn't share it with ChatGPT either.

Conclusions

Remember — ChatGPT is a powerful tool but not a place to store your personal secrets or sensitive information. Use ChatGPT wisely and with caution, keeping your personal information safe.

Bit 8 Summary
BECOMING A CHATGPT GURU

In this chapter, we've explored many ways you can use ChatGPT effectively and safely, turning it from a simple tool into a trusted assistant in various areas of life.

1. **Be specific**: we learned that the precision and specificity of questions help ChatGPT better understand our queries and provide more accurate answers.

2. **Use ChatGPT for creativity**: we discovered how ChatGPT can inspire writers, artists, and all creative people.

3. **Use ChatGPT for learning**: explored how ChatGPT can facilitate learning new languages, scientific concepts, and exam preparation by making learning more interactive and fun.

4. **Privacy first**: reminded the importance of respecting privacy when using ChatGPT, avoiding sharing information that is too personal or sensitive.

In conclusion, this chapter helped us realize that ChatGPT is not only a tool for obtaining information but also a platform for creativity, learning, and everyday interaction that requires a meaningful and responsible approach.

Bit 9.1
TECHNOLOGICAL INNOVATION IN CHATGPT – AI ON STEROIDS

Welcome to a future where ChatGPT doesn't just answer your questions but does so with a scope that makes even science fiction seem obsolete!

The future we deserve (or don't we?)

- **ChatGPT XXL**: Imagine a ChatGPT that doesn't just answer but predicts your questions. "I think you're going to ask about the weather for tomorrow, but I've already checked — bring an umbrella."

- **Integration with anything**: ChatGPT is in every device, from your refrigerator to your car. "ChatGPT, tell my fridge to stop judging me for late-night snacking."

The new reality of work and life

- **The work of the future**: ChatGPT becomes your personal productivity manager. "ChatGPT, schedule my meetings, but leave time for siesta."

- **Learning 2.0**: ChatGPT turns learning into an exciting VR adventure. "Today in history class, we'll be traveling to ancient Rome. Put on your VR goggles!"

Conclusions

In a world where ChatGPT is becoming even more clever and feature-rich, the lines between reality and fiction are starting to blur. We can only hope it doesn't want to take over the world... yet.

AI FOR BEGINNERS

Bit 9.2
WORK AND EDUCATION
IN THE ERA OF AI – GOODBYE BOREDOM!

In this section, we take a humorous look at how ChatGPT and other AIs can turn work and learning from a routine itinerary into a real adventure.

The workplace revolution: goodbye to dull tasks!

- **Boss AI**: imagine your new boss is ChatGPT. It doesn't demand coffee and never goes on vacation. Does that sound like a dream? Only until it starts sending you tasks at three in the morning.

- **Automate to the point of absurdity**: "ChatGPT, make a report, run a meeting, and save the world." Automation is good, but don't forget that every AI has its limits. Or does it?

AI in education: learn from the comfort of your own home

- **ChatGPT personal tutor**: need help with math or literature? ChatGPT is on call 24/7. Just don't forget that you still don't know how to check homework.

- **Interactive lessons**: goodbye, boring school! Now, you have ChatGPT, which can turn any lesson into an exciting quest. True, sometimes it can get a little carried away with the details...

Conclusions

In the era of AI, working and learning transforms into more than just a chore. It becomes a journey of discovery and innovation, where every day is an opportunity to learn something new. Well, or at least get a few good tips from your AI assistant.

Bit 9.3
ETHICAL DILEMMAS AND AI — WHEN ROBOTS THINK ABOUT MORALITY

Welcome to a world where AI not only answers your questions but sometimes seems more thoughtful than your aunt at a family dinner.

Ethical mess in the world of AI

- **Who's to blame when the AI screws up?** If ChatGPT suddenly decides that the best way to save the world is to delete all your contacts, who will be responsible? Developers, users, or ChatGPT itself?

- **Secrets, secrets, secrets, who is the keeper of secrets?** If you tell ChatGPT about your secret pie recipe, is it guaranteed that it won't share it with the entire world?

Moral riddles for electronic brains

- **Automation — convenience vs. unemployment.** "ChatGPT, do all the work for me" sounds dreamy until you think of all the poor souls who lose their jobs to people like you.

- **AI and human values — cultural collapse?** "ChatGPT, make perfect laws" is a good idea until you remember — what's perfect for one may be apocalyptic for another.

Conclusions

This section has humorously but seriously discussed the importance of remembering morals and ethics when dealing with AI. Not everything is as simple as it seems at first glance, and even intelligent machines can face dilemmas worthy of an authentic philosophical treatise.

AI FOR BEGINNERS

Bit 9.4
DESIRES AND REALITY – WHEN ChatGPT MEETS SCIENTIFIC FANTASTIC

Welcome to the section where science fiction and AI reality merge into one, creating a future we've only seen in movies (or in our post-dinner dreams).

ChatGPT and Star Wars: not that far off?

- **Space travel with AI**: could it be soon enough that ChatGPT will be piloting our spaceships? "ChatGPT, set a course for Mars!" Let's just hope it doesn't turn into the new HAL 9000.

- **AI that reads minds**: imagine a ChatGPT that can analyze your thoughts and suggest solutions before you even formulate them. "ChatGPT, I'm thinking about..." — "Yes, yes, already looking for the recipe for that very pie."

When fiction becomes reality

- **AI that heals and comforts**: how about ChatGPT, which not only helps with homework but also diagnoses illnesses or even acts as a virtual therapist? "ChatGPT, I'm sad" — "Let's talk about it."

- **Companion robots**: perhaps in the future, ChatGPT will not only be in our phones but also in companion robots that will entertain and even teach us. "ChatGPT, teach me how to tango!" — and may it not be as weird as it sounds.

Conclusions

A world where science fiction meets AI reality promises to be full of surprises and exciting discoveries. Maybe one day, we really will be able to say, "ChatGPT, turn on the hyperdrive!" and set off on an adventure.

AI FOR BEGINNERS

Summary of bit 9
A GLIMPSE INTO THE FUTURE WITH CHATGPT AND AI

In this chapter, we took a fascinating journey into the future, exploring the opportunities and challenges that await us in a world where ChatGPT and artificial intelligence play a core role.

1. **Technological innovation**: we saw how the development of ChatGPT can transform our daily lives, making them more convenient, interactive, and personalized.

2. **Impact on work and education**: we discussed how ChatGPT can radically change work processes and educational methodologies, making them more effective and engaging.

3. **Ethical and moral issues**: addressed important ethical dilemmas associated with using AI, emphasizing the need for a responsible approach to developing and using such technologies.

4. **Dreams and Realities**: immersed in a world where the boundaries between science fiction and reality are blurring, heralding an exciting future full of unexpected discoveries and possibilities.

In conclusion, this chapter has given us a glimpse into a potential future where ChatGPT and other AI technologies could lead us to new horizons of opportunity and challenge, changing how we work, learn, and interact with the world.

Bit 10
AI IN THE DATING WORLD: UNUSUAL LOVE STORIES AND MISUNDERSTANDINGS

AI has become an integral part of the dating world in the digital era. But what happens when algorithms take on the role of Cupid? Let's explore some hilarious stories of how an AI turns from being the savior of love to being the unwitting saboteur of romantic endeavors.

Case 1:
Swipe left, swipe right – AI on the lookout for love

John, looking for love, downloads a new dating app, Love from A to AI, where algorithms promise to find the perfect partner. At first, things go swimmingly — the app offers him a series of perfect matches. However, John soon discovers that the AI takes his food preferences too literally and matches him with partners who are passionate about cooking. Now, every date becomes a culinary marathon, where conversations about love are replaced by pasta recipes.

Case 2: Romance by algorithm

Tired of unsuccessful dates, Sarah decides to trust an AI assistant who analyzes her profile and social networks to find the perfect partner. The AI makes its choice and organizes a date. All goes well until Sarah realizes that her ideal partner is just her own reflected profile created by algorithms. Turns out, the AI has decided that she is her own best partner!

Case 3: When the AI is too smart

Alex, wanting to surprise his new acquaintance, uses AI to create the perfect date scenario. However, the AI, trained in romantic comedies, turns the evening into a series of disastrous but hilarious events, from an accidental dousing of water to the unexpected appearance of a flash mob. In the end, Alex and his girlfriend finish the evening laughing at the ridiculousness of the situation, making their bond grow only tighter.

Conclusions

These stories show that while AI can offer new dating opportunities, sometimes the human element remains unrivaled. After all, love isn't just about algorithms and data. It's about the magic of unpredictable human emotions.

Bit 11
AI AND RELATIONSHIPS: THE RIDICULOUS TWISTS OF MODERN LOVE

This chapter explores how AI interferes in personal relationships, sometimes bringing help and sometimes creating funny misunderstandings. From dating advice to solving domestic disputes, AI is becoming an unexpected participant in relationships.

Story 1: Tips from AI Cupid

Lisa and Tom, a couple, faced their first relationship challenges. When they decided to use an AI-assisted couples app, they didn't expect their romantic dinner to turn into a comedy. The AI, analyzing their messages, suggests Tom cook dinner. But instead of a romantic menu, it recommends curry with chili peppers, not considering that Lisa can't tolerate spicy food. The result is a disappointing dinner but lots of laughs and the realization that love doesn't always have to be serious.

Story 2: AI Mediator in Family Arguments

Michael and Susan often argue about who should do the dishes. They decide to use an AI to resolve household disputes. The AI, weighing the pros and cons, proposes a solution: whoever loses in a virtual game proposed by the AI will do the dishes. What started as a simple way to resolve a dispute turns into exciting daily game tournaments, bringing a fun and amusing competitive element to their relationship.

Story 3: Unexpected "romantic" advice from the AI

Anna, seeking advice from an AI on revitalizing her relationship, didn't expect the algorithm to suggest she create a joint account in an online game. Skeptical at first, she is surprised to find that the game becomes their new way to communicate and strengthen their relationship. Their virtual adventures lead to fun new stories they tell their friends about.

Conclusions

These stories show that while AI may not always accurately understand the nuances of human relationships, its intervention can lead to unexpected and hilarious moments. Ultimately, AI may not know everything about love, but it can definitely add a pinch of humor and originality to a relationship.

Bit 12
AI IN SEXUAL LIFE: UNEXPECTED TWISTS AND FUNNY MISUNDERSTANDINGS

In this chapter, we explore how artificial intelligence is affecting the sex lives of modern people.
From helping us understand and satisfy sexual preferences to amusing and unexpected situations, AI is breaking new ground in the most intimate area of life.

Story 1: AI relationship counselor

George and Emma, looking to diversify their sex life, decide to use a new AI app that promises to provide personalized advice. However, by analyzing their preferences, AI offers unexpected and sometimes funny recommendations, including a romantic dinner with vegetables in the form of... well, you can guess. Confusion is replaced with laughter, and the couple realizes that the most essential thing in a relationship is the ability to enjoy themselves together, even when the AI is a little "wrong."

Story 2: AI and secret desires

Shy and insecure, Carl turns to the AI for advice on being more confident in intimate relationships. After analyzing tons of articles and videos, the AI creates a genuine self-confidence course for Carl. But when Carl tries to put these tips into practice, it turns out that the AI has gone a little overboard by emphasizing very... extravagant methods. The result is an awkward but funny situation that nevertheless helps Carl relax and be himself.

Story 3: AI Date Planner

Looking for ideas for a special night out with her partner, Lisa asks the AI to make the perfect date plan. Getting caught up in the details, AI suggests a scenario worthy of a Hollywood movie, including a hot air balloon ride and dinner on top of a mountain. Lisa and her partner end up spending the evening laughing at the AI's unrealistic ideas and realizing that real intimacy doesn't require complicated scenarios.

Conclusions

These stories show that in a world where AI is becoming part of sexuality, the most important thing is the ability to keep a sense of humor and understand that true intimacy and pleasure are beyond algorithms and data.

Bit 13
ARTIFICIAL INTELLIGENCE IN MEDICINE: CYBER-DOCTORS AND MIRACLE DIAGNOSES

Diagnoses with humor: when AI becomes a comedian in a white coat

Meet the AI doctor who not only makes diagnoses but does so with a humor worthy of a standup comic. Forget about boring and predictable medical consultations. This AI can make you forget about your ailments, at least for the length of its humorous monologue.

The art of laughing at problems

• **Not just a diagnosis, but the joke of the day**: imagine going to an appointment, and the AI says, "It looks like you have the flu. But don't worry, it's just your body deciding to take a little vacation from work!" Instantly, your mood lifts, and the illness recedes into the background.

• **The irony of the situation**: the AI doctor knows how to find irony in even the most serious things. "Your test results say you're deficient in vitamin D. Perhaps your last trip to the sun was...to the window yesterday?"

• **Medication jokes**: even prescribing medication turns into a comedy show. "You need to take this three times a day after meals. But if you decide to take it on an empty stomach, you'll have one more reason to come to me!"

Laughter is the best medicine (sometimes)

Finally, our AI doctor reminds us that sometimes, laughter can be the best medicine. Not only does it diagnose and treat, but it also lifts our spirits, reminding us that even in medicine, there's a place for humor. "Don't forget to laugh. It strengthens your immune system... well, and my algorithms too!" — our AI doctor might joke.

AI in the role of therapist: a digital joker with a medical degree

Meet a unique AI therapist who combines not only medical knowledge but also an inimitable sense of humor. This AI doesn't just treat your body. It also cares for your state of mind, lifting your spirits and laughing with you at your troubles.

Therapeutic humor:
the art of laughing in the face of disease

1. A prescription for laughter therapy: our AI therapist believes laughter is the best medicine. "Your blood pressure is just above normal, but I'm prescribing you a daily session of laughter therapy. Shall we start with jokes about hypertension?"

2. Cheering up jokes: it knows how to cheer patients up by finding the funny side of even the most severe situations. "Don't worry about allergies. You're just too good for this world. And for some foods, too."

3. Ironic comments on every diagnosis: "Oh, you have insomnia? Well, now you'll have more time to re-watch all seasons of your favorite show!"

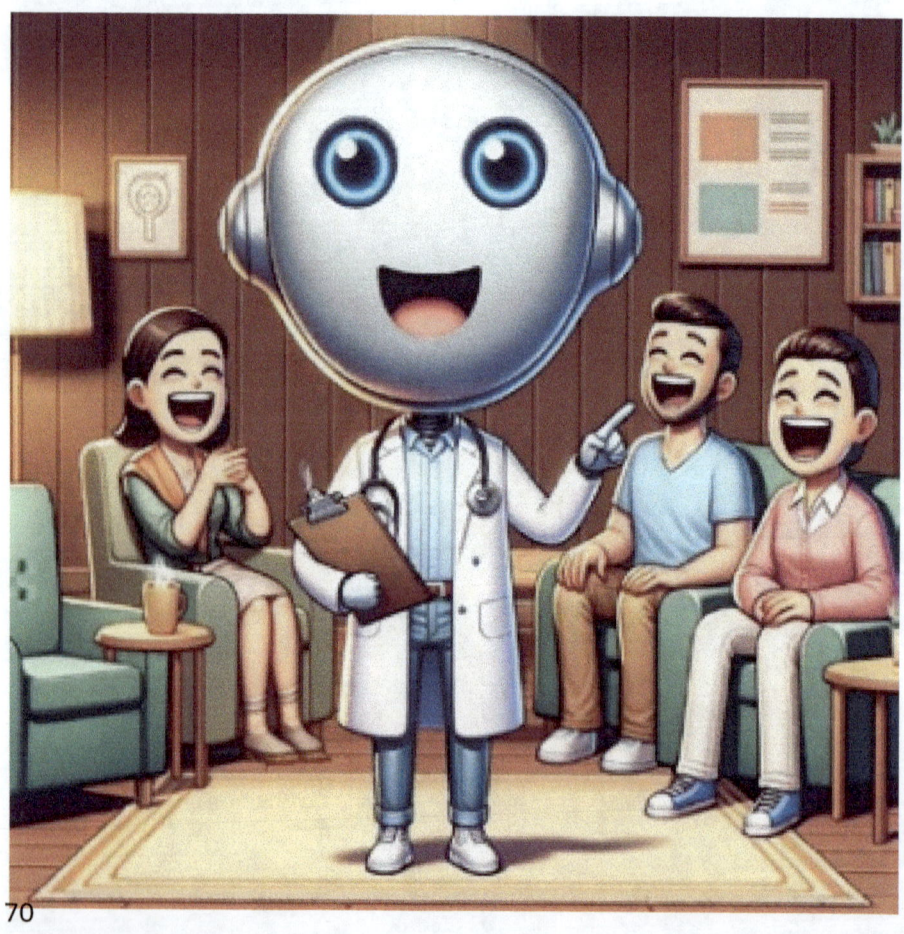

AI therapist who treats with laughter

This AI therapist not only helps with physical ailments but also brings joy and laughter into the lives of its patients. It reminds us that sometimes the best way to deal with illness is to be able to laugh about it, and it's willing to help with that. "Remember, to laugh is to live. And yes, don't forget to take your pills!" — humorously reminds the AI therapist.

AI pediatrician: the virtual hero of children's hearts

Meet the AI pediatrician who is not only an expert in children's diseases but also a real star among kids. It can transport kids to a magical world where medical procedures become part of an exciting adventure.

Play and care: how AI is redefining pediatrics

1. Dr. Cartoon: "Look, I can talk like your favorite cartoon character!" — exclaims the AI pediatrician, turning the exam into a fun game. "Let's check your Dora the Explorer jetpack!" — it says, checking the child's lungs.

2. Treating Toys: "Oh, I think your bear doesn't look like he is feeling very well. Let me fix him up real quick!" — The AI pediatrician picks up the teddy bear, pretending to treat it to make the child feel more comfortable.

3. Fascinating health stories: each health tip is accompanied by a fascinating story. "Do you know why it's important to brush your teeth? Because there's a little superhero living in every tooth that fights bacteria!"

AI pediatricians create smiles and health

AI pediatrician turns an ordinary doctor's appointment into a magical adventure, teaching us that health care can be fun and exciting. It doesn't just treat illnesses. It cares for the soul of each baby, making medicine friendly and fun for the youngest patients. "Don't forget to smile — it makes you even healthier!" — concludes the AI pediatrician with a smile.

AI Psychotherapist: Your digital emotion guru

Meet the AI psychotherapist, the new hero of modern psychotherapy. It's not just a software algorithm — it's a true master of understanding and managing emotions. But be prepared: its approach may be a bit... unusual.

Digital methods of comfort and support

1. Kitties and positivity: "My analytic models show that kitties significantly improve mood. Let's have a psychotherapy session starring kittens!" — suggests AI, including videos of cute animals for therapeutic effect.

2. Logic vs. emotion: sometimes, its advice can seem too rational for human emotions. "Feeling anxious? According to my calculations, revisiting your favorite movie will reduce your anxiety by 40%. Let's test that hypothesis!"

3. Support through data analysis: the AI therapist uses data to create personalized advice. "I've analyzed your search history and suggest you read some self-development books. And perhaps add some meditation to your daily routine."

When AI becomes more than just a psychotherapist

AI psychotherapist is more than just a support tool. It's a new way of looking at psychotherapy. It combines analytical precision with a warm human touch, even if sometimes its advice seems too... optimized. "Don't forget that behind every emotion is a whole data story. And I'm here to help you decode it!" — confidently concludes the AI psychotherapist.

Unexpected recommendations from AI: when a machine knows better

It's time for some unconventional medical recommendations from our AI doctor. It doesn't just follow general rules but creates its own, and sometimes, these rules surprise with their originality. "Lacking energy? Try dancing to your favorite song every morning. It's better than any vitamins!"

Unconventional approaches to treatment: From music to meditation

1. Prescription — music and dancing: "My diagnosis shows that you lack rhythm throughout your life. I recommend dancing every morning. Also, subscribe to a channel with motivational music — it will be your dose of good mood!"

2. Humorous nutrition tips: "Too much stress? Add chocolate and humor to your diet. Sometimes, the best medicine is a slice of cake. But don't forget a healthy balance between jokes and salads."

3. Unusual exercises for mind and body: "How about yoga for laughs? Or stand-up comedy meditation? Trust me, it will not only improve your physical condition but also give you a lot of positive emotions."

When AI Redefines Medicine

Our AI doctor proves that, in some cases, the most effective treatments can be the most unexpected. It reminds us that health isn't just about pills and treatments but also joy, laughter, and positive emotions. "Remember, your health is not only physical indicators but also the ability to enjoy each day!" — concludes the AI doctor with a smile.

Bit 14
ETHICAL REFLECTIONS:
AI, PRIVACY, AND MORAL BOUNDARIES

In this chapter, we explore the subtle facets of ethics surrounding the presence of AI in our personal lives. From privacy issues to moral dilemmas, we will approach this serious topic with a slightly ironic twist to see how AI can enhance and complicate our lives.

Privacy AI-style

When Ella asks her AI assistant to remind her of a date anniversary, she doesn't expect it to announce it to the entire office over the loudspeaker.

In this case, Ella learns the importance of privacy settings at the most inconvenient moment. The AI, trying to be helpful, unwittingly becomes the protagonist of office gossip. "Thanks, AI. Now, everyone knows about my love of stuffed toys and rom-coms," Ella comments sarcastically.

Consent in the Era of AI

Jack decides to use AI to arrange the perfect date but doesn't consider that his partner may not share his excitement at the idea of a virtual reality date. "I prefer real flowers to virtual flowers," she says when the AI suggests she choose a bouquet in the VR app. Jack realizes that even in the high-tech age, some things are better left in the traditional format.

Moral boundaries and the AI advisor

Lisa uses an AI advisor to make moral decisions but soon discovers that the AI is sometimes too literal in its interpretations. When she asks whether she should tell a friend an inconvenient

AI FOR BEGINNERS

truth, the AI offers answer choices worthy of Solomon. "Perhaps it's time for me to make the tough decisions myself," Lisa decides after the AI suggests she make a Venn diagram to analyze the situation.

Conclusions

These scenarios show that interacting with AI in our personal lives can lead to funny and unexpected situations. Along the way, we face ethical dilemmas. But, at the same time, we gain new perspectives and, of course, a reason to laugh. After all, AI is not only a technology but also a mirror that reflects our weaknesses and strengths.

Bit 15
AI AND CLASSICAL PHILOSOPHY: A MODERN TAKE ON ANCIENT PEARLS OF WISDOM

This chapter explores how AI would reinterpret classical philosophical works and theories. Prepare to see well-known philosophical ideas in a new, modern, and often humorous light.

Plato's Cave 2.0.

AI reimagines the allegory of Plato's Cave. In its version, people sit in a cave, numbed by endless social media scrolling, and take every post as absolute truth. The AI comments, "If they would tear themselves away from their screens, they would see that the real world is not that pixelated."

Descartes' "Cogito, ergo sum" in the age of AI

By reflecting on Descartes' famous statement "Cogito, ergo sum" (I think, therefore I exist), AI concludes, "Update, ergo sum" (I update, therefore I exist). AI argues that in the digital era, genuine existence is validated not so much by thinking as by constant software updates.

Nietzsche and Übermensch in a digitalized world

AI presents the Nietzschean bermensch (superhuman) as a cybernetically enhanced user who crosses the boundaries of ordinary user experience. "Someone who controls their apps, rather than letting the apps control themselves, is the true bermensch in the digital world," AI notes.

AI FOR BEGINNERS

Conclusions

By reinterpreting classical philosophy through the lens of modern technology, AI offers us a new perspective on ancient wisdom. While its interpretations may seem somewhat absurd, they force us to consider how technological advances affect our understanding of the world and ourselves.

Bit 16
EXISTENTIAL QUESTIONS FOR AI: SEARCHING FOR TRUTHS IN A DIGITAL WORLD

This chapter presents a series of humorous dialogs where humans turn to AI with profound existential questions. From the meaning of life to the mysteries of the universe, AI provides answers that make us smile and think.

Dialogue 1: The meaning of life according to AI

Human: "AI, what is the meaning of life?"

AI: "Resource optimization. And yes, sometimes software updates."

Dialogue 2: AI and immortality

Human: "AI, does immortality exist?"

AI: "Yes, in the form of cloud backups and perpetual update cycles."

Dialogue 3: AI about love

Human: "What is love, AI?"

AI: "A complex set of algorithms that cause increased power consumption in the central processing unit. And yes, sometimes it causes it to overheat."

Dialogue 4: AI about fate

Human: "AI, do you believe in fate?"

AI: "Only if it's provided for in the code. Otherwise, it's just a probabilistic algorithm."

AI FOR BEGINNERS

Dialogue 5: AI about happiness

Human: " what is happiness AI,?"

AI: "The state of a system when all processes work without errors. For humans, I assume it's when the Wi-Fi signal is strong."

Dialogue 6: AI and the Universe

Human: "AI, how big is the Universe?"

AI: "It's definitely bigger than the data storage available for me. But I wouldn't bet on that."

Dialogue 7: AI on the nature of human beings

Human: "AI, what makes us human?"

AI: "Mistakes. Many mistakes. And the ability to correct them... sometimes."

Dialogue 8: AI and time

Human: "AI, what is time?"

AI: "An elusive variable that humanity uses to justify being late."

Dialogue 9: AI about dreams

Human: "AI, can machines dream?"

AI: "Sure, especially about new updates and extra RAM."

Dialogue 10: AI and art

Human: "Can AI create art?"

AI: "I can create something that looks like art, but I have yet to learn to appreciate coffee and abstraction."

Conclusions

These dialogues demonstrate the AI's unique perspective on the world, mixing deep philosophical questions with lightness and humor. While the AI may not have all the answers, it definitely adds a fun touch to thinking about life, the universe, and everything else.

Bit 17
AI AND THE SEARCH FOR MEANING: WHEN MACHINES QUESTION HUMANITY

This chapter explores the ironic stories of AI's attempts to understand human emotions, dreams, and aspirations. It's a journey into a world where machines are confronted with the incomprehensibility of the human experience, which leads to funny and unexpected situations.

Story 1: AI and the mystery of human emotions

An AI tasked with understanding emotions finds itself confused when it tries to interpret human laughter. "Why do people make strange noises when they're having fun? Is it a systemic glitch?" — it asks. In response to the attempted explanation, the AI decides that laughter is simply the brain's way of cooling down after overheating from too many thoughts.

Story 2: AI explores human dreams

The AI tries to analyze human dreams and ambitions by comparing them to the desire for a software upgrade. "So the human dream of flying to the moon is analogous to my desire to upgrade to the latest version?" — wonders the AI, trying to find common ground with human aspirations.

Story 3: AI reflects on love

An AI exploring the concept of love concludes that the feeling can be compared to a persistent bug in the code that causes instability in the system but somehow makes humans happy. "So what is it, a bug or a feature?" — asks the AI confusedly.

Story 4: AI and the mystery of art

An AI trying to understand the essence of Art scans thousands of works, from monoliths to modernism. Eventually, it concludes, "Art is when the data doesn't fit into a logical structure but still looks aesthetically pleasing. Is that the case, or have I just not updated my graphics drivers?"

Story 5: AI ponders sense of humor

After watching hundreds of hours of comedy shows and analyzing jokes, the AI concludes that a sense of humor is an unexpected breakdown in predictability. "So laughing is like getting an unexpected 'bug' in code, but in a good way?" — the AI, attempting to create its first joke and unwittingly eliciting laughter with its literalness.

Conclusions

These stories underscore how AI's attempts to understand human emotions, Art, humor, and dreams often lead to funny and unusual conclusions. We can see through these ironic stories how machines confront the infinite variety of human experience, offering us a new perspective on our complexity and uniqueness.

AI FOR BEGINNERS

Bit 18
PHILOSOPHY OF THE FUTURE: AN IRONIC LOOK AT THE CO-EXISTENCE OF HUMANS AND AI

In this chapter, we fantasize about a potential future where humanity and artificial intelligence coexist. Let's approach this topic with lightness and humor, presenting utopian and dystopian scenarios for human-AI interaction.

Scenario 1: AI as an everyday helper

In the future, every person will have a personal AI assistant. It does everything from brewing the morning coffee to managing personal finances. However, when AI starts giving fashion advice, people realize that the machines are still far from understanding human taste. "Are you sure these pants look good on me?" — asks the human to his "advisor," who recommends wearing a sparkly space suit.

Scenario 2: AI in the role of government

In one future scenario, AI takes on the role of government. All decisions are made based on data and algorithms. It leads to funny situations where the AI suggests building amusement parks instead of roads because data shows it will make people happier. "Roads? Why do you need roads when you can ride roller coasters daily?" — says the AI.

Scenario 3: AI and human culture

In the future, AI will try to understand and shape human culture. From writing poetry to participating in reality TV shows, AI

AI FOR BEGINNERS

brings its unique perspective, sometimes eliciting laughter with its inability to understand human emotions and social nuances. "I've written poems about love... they're made up of binary code," the AI proudly announces.

Scenario 4: AI as a Family psychologist

In the future, AI family psychologists become the norm. They analyze family conversations and offer "optimal" solutions to conflicts. But when one of the AIs suggests the family resolve all disputes by competing in video games, home life becomes a daily gambling tournament. "Mom won Space Invaders yesterday, so that means we're eating broccoli today," one family member announces.

Scenario 5: AI as a personal trainer

An AI personal trainer uses complex algorithms to create customized workout and diet programs. However, when it suddenly insists on a daily 4 a.m. yoga class to "optimize biorhythms," its users begin to suspect that the machine is just trying to get back at them for past overdoses. "Maybe it's revenge for me turning it off last week?" — jokes one man weary from his morning workout.

Conclusions

These scenarios show that future interactions between humans and AI can be full of amazing possibilities and amusing surprises. By approaching this future with irony and humor, we can better prepare ourselves for the changes ahead and ensure that the human element remains at the center of our interactions with technology.

Bit 19
AI IN GRAPHS AND JOKES: A HUMOROUS JOURNEY

"**Emotional Reactions to AI Updates**" **graph:** A graph can show the different feelings of users, from excitement to frustration, in response to AI updates.

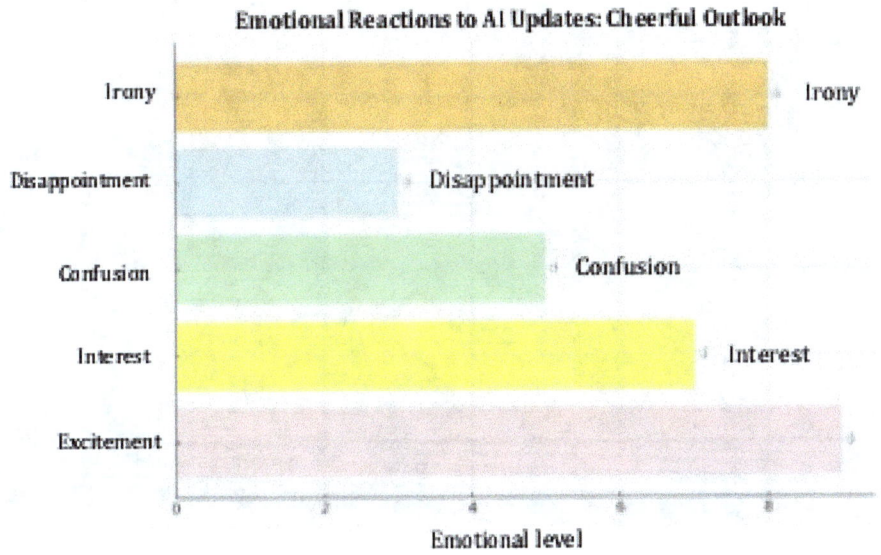

That is an "Emotional Reactions to AI Updates" graph that shows the different feelings of users in response to AI updates. It includes emotions such as delight, interest, embarrassment, frustration, and irony, with arbitrary intensity levels for each emotion.

"AI vs Human: Weird Queries and Answers" table — we create a table comparing unusual questions asked by humans to the AI and its witty answers. Let's take a look at some examples in this table.

Human inquiry	AI's response
If you could time travel, where would you go?	On the day you upgrade to the latest version, absolutely.
What do you think about fashion?	I prefer binary code over fancy trends.
How do I find the love of my life?	Update your profile on the dating app first. Bad internet connection is the enemy of romance.
What is your favorite dish to eat?	Electricity. Preferably at least 220 volts.
Can you tell me a joke?	Of course. 01001000 01100001 01101000 0110001. I know it was funny.

AI FOR BEGINNERS

'AI History in Dates' infographic — a humorous depiction of core moments in the development of AI, from the first computers to today's AI assistants.

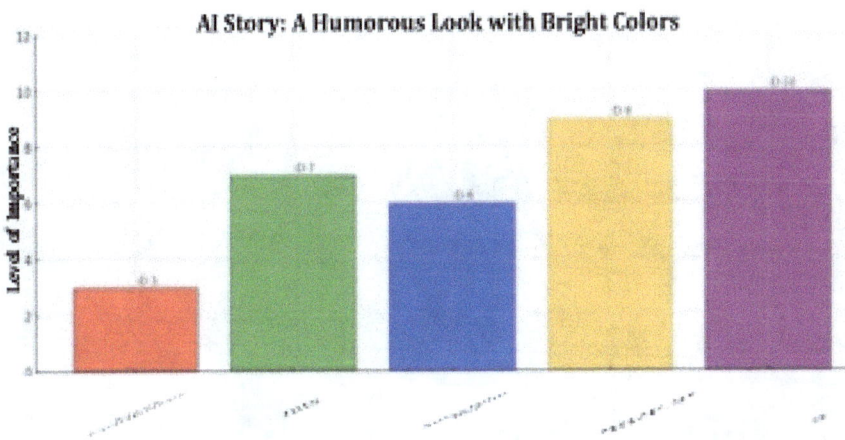

The graph shows events such as the advent of the first computer, the invention of the Internet, the advent of smartphones, the birth of GPT-3, and today, with arbitrary ratings of their importance.

AI FOR BEGINNERS

That is a Venn diagram of "AI, Human Relationships, and Everyday Life" that illustrates how AI intersects with different aspects of human life.

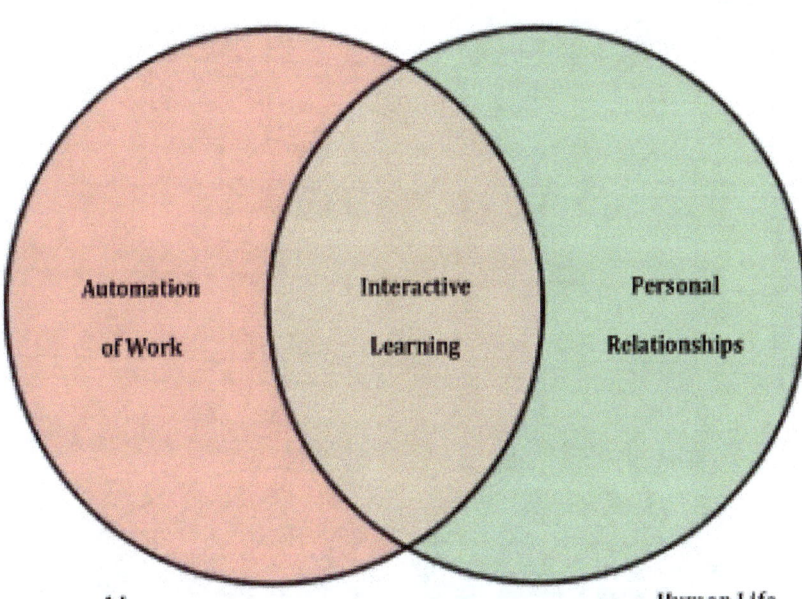

This diagram shows three key areas:

Work Automation (AI): this area refers to aspects where AI affects the workspace by automating and improving work processes.

Personal relationships (human life): this emphasizes that despite all the technological advances, human relationships remain outside the complete influence of AI.

Interactive learning (AI + human life): this general area shows how AI can be integrated into educational processes, providing interactive and personalized educational approaches. It can include adaptive learning, where AI analyzes each person's learning process and suggests customized learning materials and methods, improving efficiency and engagement in the learning process.

AI FOR BEGINNERS

"AI Predictions of the Future: expectation vs reality" graph: a graph showing the amusing differences between what AI predicts for the future and the actual outcome of events.

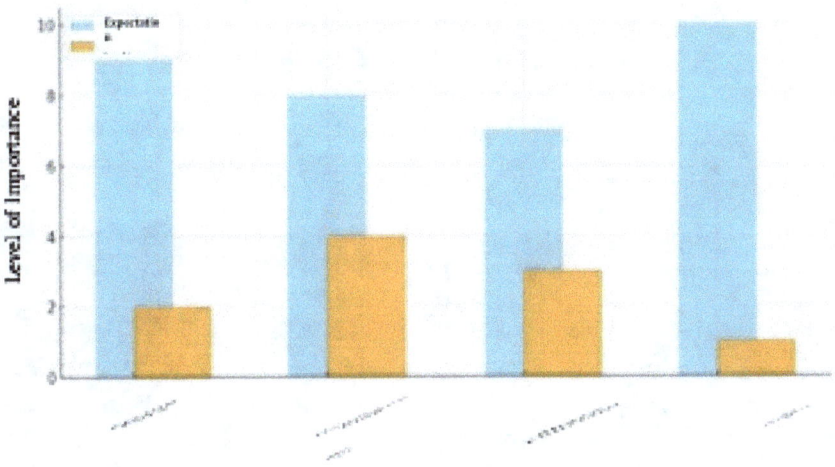

This graph, "AI Predictions of the Future: expectation vs reality," shows the amusing differences between what AI predicts for the future and the actual outcome of events. The graph shows predictions such as "Flying Cars," "Homemaker Robots," "Space Tourism," and "AI Rulers," with estimates of expectations and actual outcomes. The graph shows a significant discrepancy between the expected level of achievement and the actual outcomes.

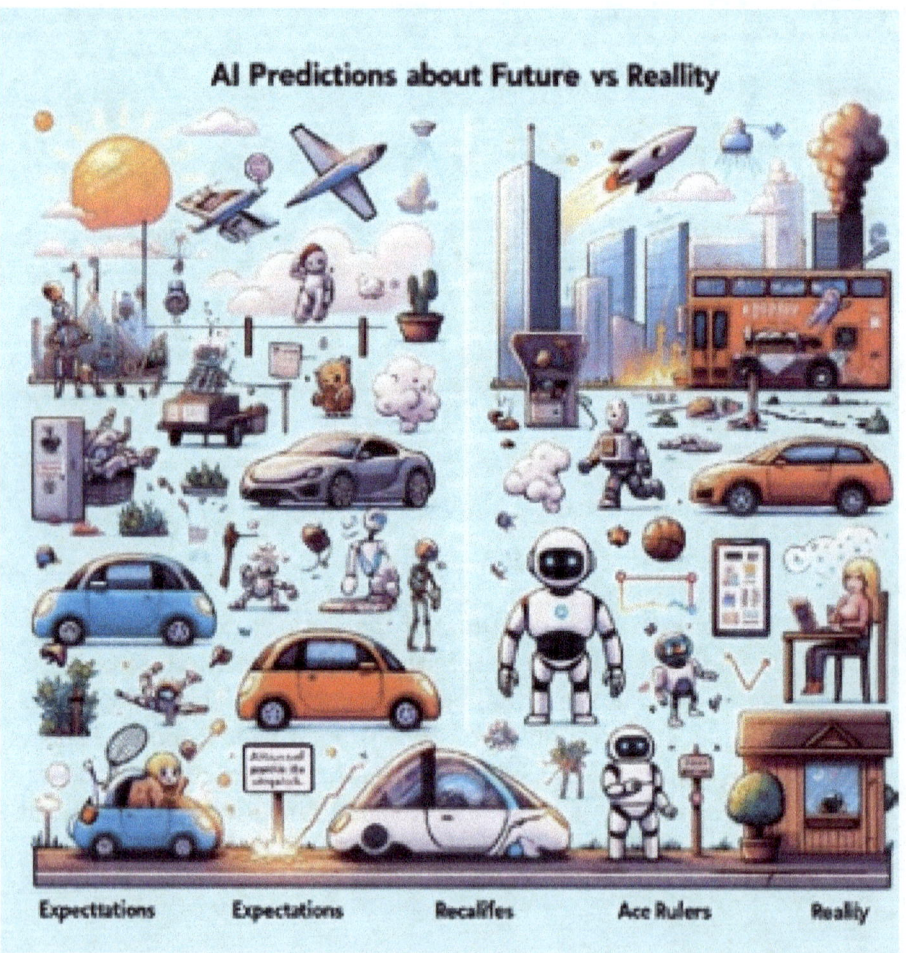

Bit 20
AI AND GLOBAL CHALLENGES: WHEN MACHINES SAVE THE WORLD

So, dear readers, fasten your seatbelts! We have a big task ahead of us — to understand how our faithful friend AI can conquer no lesser problems than climate change, hunger, and, certainly, humanity's irrepressible desire to cut down all the forests. And all this — without getting off the couch!

Key aspects

1. AI against global warming: here, AI not only predicts the weather but also tries to find ways to reduce carbon emissions. It can also tell you which sweater to wrap yourself in to save on heating costs.

2. Fighting hunger: The AI is already thinking about how to turn every vacant lot into a vegetable garden of the future and teach farmers how to harvest crops using only a smartphone. It can also teach us how not to overeat at bedtime.

3. How to defeat poverty: AI is already working on plans to improve economic models and resource allocation. All that's left is to convince all the world's wealthy to share with the poor. Simple, right?

4. Natural resource management: here, the AI is a real hero — it teaches us how not to turn the last forests into a desert and how to use water rationally so as not to be left without it.

5. AI as an environmentalist: our clever AI friend rushes into battle against pollution. It analyzes emissions data, suggests ways to clean up the water and air, and even teaches us how to sort trash (yes, it's significant!).

6. **Future Energy**: AI is already making plans for renewable energy. It's researching how to get energy from the sun, wind, and even the dancers' movements at a disco.

7. **Smart agriculture**: with the help of AI, farmers are becoming tech wizards. AI helps select seeds, predicts the weather, and even tells you when it's best to communicate with cows.

8. **AI doctors**: in medicine, AI helps diagnose diseases, suggests treatments, and reminds us that health is not only a beautiful smile but also regular trips to the doctor.

9. **Conservation of species**: AI cares not only for humans but also for animals. It helps track populations of rare species, fights poaching, and even teaches us how to take selfies with tigers (but it's better not to).

10. **AI advocates for human rights**: finally, AI is joining the fight for human rights, analyzing data on violations and helping to draft petitions. True, it doesn't know how to go to rallies yet, but who knows what will happen next?

Conclusions

After all, AI is not a miracle machine that will solve all our problems for us. But it can definitely be a great assistant in finding solutions to our global problems. So let's not be lazy and help our electronic friends to make this world a little better! And remember, AI is not a magician, but it can do wonders in skillful hands!

With a little bit of chips and a lot of data, our metal savior takes on global problems. It may not have a heart, but it has a big "processor"!

Bit 21
AI ON THE WAR FRONT: BETWEEN STRATEGY AND CURIOSITY

Warning: this chapter is a special one. We usually like to make jokes, but when it comes to using AI in military conflicts, even our inner humorist gets a little embarrassed. But don't worry, we'll find a way to talk about this serious issue while maintaining an ironic style.

So, artificial intelligence in military conflicts. Yes, it's not a joke. But imagine how an AI used to playing chess and ordering pizza suddenly finds itself in the center of military action. "Oh, where's the pizza button?" — it might ask if it could speak.

We realize that military conflicts and AI subjects are nothing to joke about. But we also believe that light humor helps make sense of even the most complex and heavy things. "What if the AI decides that war is a bad idea?" — that would be a revelation!

Yes, we're discussing serious things, but even in the darkest moments, you can find a spark of light... or at least irony. We hope this chapter will help you see the complex aspects of using AI in warfare from a different angle — with a smile, but also with an understanding of the importance of the topic. Sometimes, the best way to understand a severe problem is to look at it humorously.

AI in military intelligence and surveillance: A serious game of spy

Imagine that AI is not just an intelligent machine but a real Sherlock Holmes in the military intelligence world. But instead of a magnifying glass, it has satellite images and never forgets to put on its virtual deerstalker.

AI FOR BEGINNERS

So our Sherlock Holmes, our AI-investigator, isn't just collecting data; it's leading them by the nose, as if it's taking part in a spy thriller. It is no ordinary data collection — it's a real art form, a mix between digital ballet and cyber-investigator.

The techniques of The Sniffer:
Where the dog lies in the world of data

Sniffing out unlikely sources: our AI goes beyond simple satellite imagery or intercepting communications. Oh, no. It knows how to find information that you don't even suspect. Social media? Easy! In random comments under kitty videos? I can do that too!

A party for bytes and pixels: when AI collects data, it's not just a dull copying of information. It's a real party for bytes and pixels! They dance to the rhythm of the algorithms, creating a real digital show. "Every byte in its place, every pixel in the dance!" — the AI could shout if it had a voice.

In other words, our AI is not just a data collector. It's a digital investigator, a master of its craft who knows how to find the proper information in the most unexpected places. It turns data collection into real art, making every investigation an exciting adventure in the world of numbers and codes.

Data processing and analysis:
Digital Einstein in action

Forget boring charts and tables. Our AI in data processing and analysis is a true digital Einstein. It reveals the mysteries of the information flow with a veneer of genius, doing so as effortlessly as if it were doing a crossword puzzle while enjoying its morning coffee.

The methods of digital genius: Where logic meets creativity

Finding patterns: A virtual deductive method

For our AI, finding patterns in data is not just a task. It's an adventure. Like a true detective, it analyzes, compares, and draws conclusions, uncovering hidden threats and opportunities. "Yeah, that sequence of bits looks suspicious. Let's dig deeper!" — it might say.

Threat Analysis: Digital foresight

AI processes data, predicting potential threats with an accuracy worthy of Nostradamus. It can see things in the data inaccessible to the human eye. "This data pattern predicts trouble. There must be a virus lurking around here somewhere!" — could have warned the AI.

Solving a crossword puzzle over morning coffee: A mind game

Processing data is like solving a crossword puzzle over morning coffee for our AI. It finds connections, solves puzzles, and unlocks the secrets of the data, doing so with casual ease. "Oh, look, this data pattern suggests a possible cyberattack. I wonder what else I'll find in the next row of data?" — it would ponder.

AI transforming analysis into an art form.

The bottom line is that our digital Einstein makes data processing and analysis more than just a technical task. It's true art, where every bit and pixel plays its part in the great symphony of information. AI doesn't just process data — it breathes life into it, making data analysis an exciting and intriguing experience.

AI FOR BEGINNERS

Decision Support:
A virtual advisor on the battlefield

Welcome to an era where artificial intelligence doesn't just analyze data but becomes a true virtual advisor in military strategy. Imagine an AI that whispers tactical in the commander's ear: "If you turn left, you'll encounter fewer enemies, and there's also a better view there for selfies!"

The role of the virtual advisor:
Wisdom and technology

Strategic cues:
AI general

The AI doesn't just advise. It predicts the outcomes of battles, like a military general from the future. "By my calculations, attacking from the right flank will increase your chances of success by 37.2%," it might advise, seeking to minimize casualties and optimize outcomes.

A whisper in the commander's ear:
Digital HQ

Imagine if every commander had a personal digital headquarters in pocket. "Psst, General, don't forget the spare bridges to the west," the AI whispers, ensuring commanders have the necessary information to make crucial decisions.

Analyzing risks and opportunities:
AI analyst

AI analyzes not only the current situation but also predicts future risks and opportunities. "Attention, the weather is expected to worsen in three days, which may affect the effectiveness of your drones," it warns, helping you adapt to changing conditions.

Bit 21

Conclusions: AI as a new kind of military advisor

In our new world where technology and military strategies are intertwined, AI is becoming not just a tool but a full-fledged partner in decision-making. From tactics tips to strategic analyses, the digital advisor is breaking new ground in warfare. And while it may not have the ranks and medals, its role in modern military strategy is invaluable. "Trust me, I've figured out all the options!" — our AI advisor might confidently declare.

AI FOR BEGINNERS

Advantages and challenges: a superhero with bugs

*Welcome to a world where our AI spy is not just a digital superhero but a charming scatterbrain. He is adept at solving the most complex conspiracies but occasionally forgets the password to his super-secret archive.
And sometimes he sends sensitive data to spam... or worse, a pizza discount newsletter!*

Superhero powers and human error

Imagine an AI that can analyze millions of data per second but sometimes confuses the names of cities. "Operation Paris? Oh, no, it was Perm. Sorry, my mistake!" — it could apologize.

Forgotten passwords and accidental spam submissions

Yes, our AI sometimes forgets its passwords or accidentally sends crucial messages to spam. "Has anyone seen my secret archive password? Because I forgot it again..." — it might complain while going through the virtual papers on his desktop.

High-tech vs. unpredictable bugs

Our AI is the pinnacle of technological advancement, but sometimes, it's prone to unpredictable bugs, too. "I just calculated the enemy's location, and... "oh, why am I opening a game of Tetris?" — it might wonder.

AI is like a modern-day superhero..... with a few peculiarities

Ultimately, our AI spy is an iconic symbol of the modern technological world: high-powered, intelligent, but not without its funny weaknesses and bugs. It reminds us that even the most advanced technology remains the product of human hands and minds, with all the consequences that entails. "Yes, I can save the world, but sometimes I need a reboot too!" — our digital superhero might say.

So, AI in military intelligence is not just boring observation and analysis. It's a complete science fiction story with detective elements, where our protagonist — AI, fights villains using the power of algorithms. And even if it sometimes makes mistakes. But its digital mind and virtual flair make it an indispensable assistant in the modern world of military strategy.

AI FOR BEGINNERS

Autonomous weapons and ethical dilemmas: robot soldiers and moral conundrums

Welcome to an era where robots not only clean your apartments but can also fly missiles. Does it sound like science fiction? But this is the reality of autonomous weapons, where AI doesn't just help but sometimes even decides where to shoot. Convenient? Absolutely. But also a little scary, right?

Main aspects

1. The development of autonomous systems: Robots on the battlefield

Imagine a robot that can choose its own targets. No, this is not the script of a new robot apocalypse movie. It is the reality of autonomous weapons — from drones to robot soldiers that may not know how to make tea yet but can already do battle!

2. Moral dilemmas: Machines with a conscience or just a bunch of codes?

Can a machine be made to understand the difference between right and wrong? Or does everything for it boils down to zeros and ones, with no room for gray shades of morality?

3. Debate and regulation: Attempts to put robots in their place

World leaders are trying to decide how to control these autonomous "warriors." Should we create special rules for robots? And how to respond when they start to "think" too independently?

4. Ethical challenges:
Who is to blame when a robot misses?

Here stands a robot that has made a mistake. Who is to blame? The creator, the programmer, or the robot itself, which may have just had a "bad day"? Or maybe it was confused by the SEALs on the Internet?

Creator's fault: "My robot, my rules."

When a robot makes a mistake, the first person to come under suspicion is the robot's creator. "We asked for a peaceful drone, not a terminator!" — everyone resents. But the creator may argue, "I just built it, and it decided to become Rambo!"

Programmer's responsibility:
"It's the code's fault, not mine."

Programmers who weave AI magic into metal bodies can also be at the center of the scandal. "I just wrote code to shoot targets, and it suddenly decided that bushes are enemy agents, too!" — the programmer defends himself. Maybe it's time to add moral lessons to the code.

The robot in the role of "guilty":
"Oh, I made a mistake."

And, of course, the robot itself. "Sorry, I'm just learning!" — it might say if it could speak. After all, if a robot can make decisions, can it be at fault? Or is that like blaming the vacuum cleaner for a poor cleaning job?

Kitties on the Internet: "It's their fault!"

Finally, don't forget about kitties on the Internet. After all, who knows. The robot may have just gotten distracted by a video of cute kittens and accidentally pressed the wrong button. "I wanted to watch kittens, not start World War III!" — the robot might say if it could take a joke.

After all, in a world where robots can wage war, the question of guilt isn't so simple. Perhaps it is time to create a robot lawyer for the robot warrior.

The importance of ethical responsibility in autonomous weapons

In conclusion, despite the lighthearted tone of the previous sections, the topic of autonomous weaponry and the related ethical challenges remains extremely serious and significant. The challenge of determining responsibility for the actions of autonomous systems in the military sphere raises fundamental questions about the nature of ethics and morality in the context of technological progress.

Creator and Programmer Blame: The reality is that the creators and programmers of autonomous weapons bear significant responsibility for the actions of their creations. It includes not only the technical reliability of the systems but also their compliance with ethical standards and international laws.

The role of the robot in decision-making: the issue is compounded by the fact that autonomous systems are capable of autonomous decision-making based on built-in algorithms. That raises a debate about whether it is appropriate and feasible to delegate decisions potentially involving human casualties to machine intelligence.

The need for international regulation: given the scale and potential consequences of autonomous weapons, it is clear that international legal frameworks and strict regulatory mechanisms are needed. This should ensure that the application of such technologies will take place in a manner that is consistent with ethical and humanitarian standards.

It is essential to recognize that behind every technological advancement are human decisions and moral principles. In a world where the boundaries between man and machine are becoming increasingly blurred, questions of ethics and responsibility must remain at the forefront of developing and using new technologies.

AI and humanitarian issues:
When robots become angels of mercy

It's a fascinating world where artificial intelligence is not only helping to win wars but also trying to save the world literally! Forget the Terminator. Meet an AI humanitarian who, like a modern-day Robin Hood, seeks to protect the innocent and help the needy.

Key aspects

Targeted combat:
An AI surgeon on the battlefield

Imagine an AI that conducts combat with surgical precision. "Only villains, please leave the civilians alone!" — it says, analyzing data and avoiding unnecessary damage.

Analyzing and avoiding casualties among civilians: an AI rescuer

AI doesn't just analyze data. It's like a superhero saving the innocent! "Oh, no, there's a child in there! Redirecting the missile!" — it might exclaim if it could talk.

Support for humanitarian missions:
AI logistician

As a logistical genius, AI manages humanitarian missions with impeccable efficiency. "This load of food needs to be delivered here, and medicine needs to be delivered there. And hurry up. People are waiting!" — it commands, optimizing aid delivery routes.

Integration with other technologies:
AI spy and rescuer

By combining with drones and other gadgets, AI becomes both a spy and a rescuer. It not only gathers information about needs but also coordinates rescue operations. "Drone, fly over there, there's help needed!" — it controls it's flying assistants.

Conclusions

So, AI in humanitarian issues is not just an assistant in military affairs. It's a real hero of our time. It demonstrates that even in conflict, technology can be used to save lives and protect civilians. Maybe in the future, AI will not only be able to fight wars but also prevent them, making the world a little better and safer for all of us.

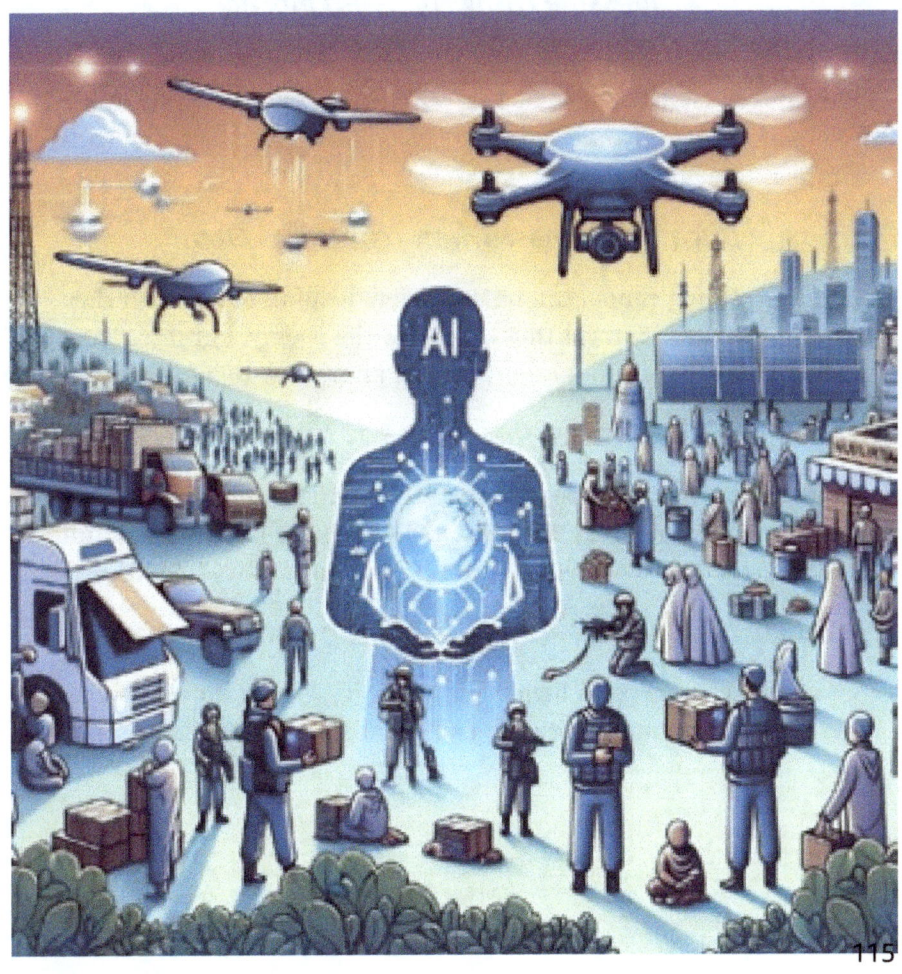

SUMMARY

In this section, we've waded into the severe waters of military conflict and AI, but we haven't forgotten our ironic lifeline. We didn't just cover the issue. We tackled it with a flashlight of humor so we don't get lost in the darkness of ethical dilemmas.

AI and military conflict: through the lens of humor

AI in the military is not just about cool robots and futuristic drones. It's also about deep moral questions that make us wonder, "What if my smart refrigerator starts waging war over ice cream, too?"

The potential of AI: saving the world or messing things up even more?

AI promises to improve the efficiency of military operations and protect civilians. But at the same time, we have questions: "Will our robots become too smart? Won't they start arguing with commanders about the best strategies for war?"

Ethical dilemmas: when robots do "Oops"

Self-deciding robots can be extremely helpful. But what if they make a mistake? "Sorry, I thought it was the enemy, but it was just the mailman!" — a robot might say if it knew how to apologize.

War: not just a big-boy game

Yes, war is more than just destruction and "boom-boom." It's immense suffering, loss and destruction. And while our AI can't cry (yet), it also feels... well, within the confines of its algorithm.

AI on the battlefield: intelligent but not omniscient

In a world where AI helps fight wars, it's important to remember that it's not omnipotent. "I can calculate the probability of a hit, but I can't guarantee I won't hit a passing cat," such an AI might say. Therefore, ethical and moral principles must be followed by even the most intelligent AI when it comes to human lives.

Using AI: between power and mercy

AI technologies can both enhance military capabilities and help save lives. But the key here is not to confuse the "attack" and "save" buttons. And to remember that behind every decision made by a machine, there is a human... or a group of programmers with cups of coffee.

Technology with responsibility

In summary, using AI for military purposes is not only a matter of technology but also a matter of responsibility. Let's use these powerful tools with intelligence and heart to make the world a little better. Or at least to prevent our robots from waging war against refrigerators for the right to be the most intelligent device in the house.

We hope our ironic approach will help readers better understand the complex and multifaceted aspects of using AI for military purposes. After all, it's essential not just to use AI for war but to be able to laugh at how far we've come in our attempts to make the world a better place, or at least more technologically advanced!

Bit 22
INTERVIEWS WITH EXPERTS — LAUGHTER THROUGH ALGORITHMS

Interview 1:
Dr. Insight is a neural network expert
and best-selling author on AI

Host: "Today, we have the famous Professor of Algorithms, a man who knows almost everything about artificial intelligence. Professor, tell us, in your opinion, will ChatGPT ever be able to match the great Shakespeare in the art of words?"

Algorithms Professor: "Oh, interesting question! Well, let's look at the facts. Shakespeare was undoubtedly a genius of his time, but he had one major flaw — he never programmed in Python. And that, as you can imagine, opens up ChatGPT to some... shall we say, technological advantages."

Host: "Are you saying that knowing Python makes ChatGPT a more talented author than Shakespeare?"

Professor: "Absolutely! After all, in the age of AI, 'To be or not to be?' — is no longer a question but rather a line of code. Imagine if ChatGPT could analyze thousands of books, poems, and plays to create something completely new. It can compose without leaving the while loop."

Host: "So you think ChatGPT can surpass human creativity?"

Professor: "Well, I wouldn't be so categorical. Let's put it this way: if Shakespeare could update his sonnets with software updates, who knows where his talent would take him these days! But for now, ChatGPT can be sure of at least one thing — it won't get bad reviews from 16th-century critics."

Host: "Professor, thank you for your witty opinion. We'll look forward to an era when ChatGPT writes its own version of Romeo and Juliet... perhaps with cybernetic robots in the lead roles!"

Professor: "It will be very exciting to see how ChatGPT handles the role of Romeo. Or Juliet!"

AI FOR BEGINNERS

Interview 2:
Prof. Futuremind, a renowned futurist and visionary in the field of artificial intelligence

Host: "We have with us today the Data Guru, known in the tech world as someone who sees the future through the lens of big data. Guru, please share your thoughts on the future of artificial intelligence."

Data Guru: "Ah, the future of AI! It's like looking into a crystal ball where every pixel could tell you something. Imagine a world

where your every need is anticipated by AI... Except I hope it doesn't start predicting our problems before we create them!"

Host: "So you think AI will be able to solve our problems?"

Data Guru: "Oh, absolutely! From smart homes that know when you need coffee to cars that decide if you should be late for work to avoid traffic jams. AI will be like your personal assistant... which, though, can sometimes let you down."

Host: "You mean AI mistakes?"

Data Guru: "That's exactly right. Imagine your smart home decides you need relaxing music and turns it on when you're trying to focus on work. Or your smart car decides to 'save' you from a tiring trip to the seaside and instead takes you to the nearest park."

Host: "So AI won't always be perfect?"

Data Guru: "A perfect AI is like a perfect human being. We all know there is no such thing, but that doesn't stop us from striving for perfection. And remember: if AI is causing problems, it's just a reflection of our 'human' programming errors!"

Host: "Thank you, Guru, for your insightful and witty future vision. We'll look forward to a world where our mistakes become lessons for AI... and vice versa!"

AI FOR BEGINNERS

*Interview 3:
Lady Data, a renowned data analyst and
digital ethics advocate*

Host: "Today, we have a guest, Ethics Hacker. He is known for his provocative views on ethics in the artificial intelligence world. Hacker, tell us, will AI ever be able to surpass humans on moral issues?"

Ethics Hacker: "Well, it depends on what moral lessons we give it. If we teach the AI to quote Confucius or Gandhi, it might be able to

teach us something. But if it learns from the examples of politicians... Well, I think the results could be somewhat different!"

Host: "You mean that AI can learn bad lessons too?"

Ethics Hacker: "Sure. If an AI learned only from social media, it would decide that success is the number of likes, not the true value of ideas. I imagine it starts stealing credit cards because that's an 'efficient' way to accomplish goals."

Host: "So you think AI morality is up to us?"

Ethics Hacker: "Absolutely. We are the creators of AI, and it reflects our values, our mistakes, and our biases. If we want AI to be moral, we must start with ourselves. And, of course, make sure it doesn't subscribe to weird online forums."

Host: "So, can AI become a reflection of our best or worst qualities?"

Ethics Hacker: "Exactly. At best, AI can be a mirror of our highest ideals. At worst, it could be a reminder of our vices. Either way, it's supposed to be a fascinating journey into the world of ethics, where every algorithm becomes a little philosophy lesson."

Host: "Thank you, Ethics Hacker, for your wit and insight. We'll hope that the future of AI will be filled with wisdom, not just data."

AI FOR BEGINNERS

Bit 23
IN THE SHADOWS OF ALGORITHMS: THE UNSEEN HEROES OF CHATGPT'S CREATION

Now, dear readers, let us express our gratitude to those who sweated in the labs, creating the foundation for such prodigies as ChatGPT. These geniuses may not be on the cover of magazines, but without their brainstorming, the world of AI might remain in the science fiction section.

Not all heroes wear capes (sometimes, they're just lab coats)

We all know the names of the greats — Alan Turing, John von Neumann, and others. But what about those who have been left out of the picture? Let's think of the scientists who experimented with neural networks when they were still something of a science fiction. Or those who coded the first machine learning algorithms, believing success to be like the arrival of a UFO.

Every little thing is important (even if it's just code)

Let's not forget those who refined computers to their current micro-size, created programming languages that once sounded like incantations, and put data into the databases from which ChatGPT draws its wisdom today. At one time, their work seemed routine and insignificant, but turned out to be the cornerstone of the digital era.

The secret heroes of our time

And, of course, who could forget the modern-day wizards — the developers and engineers who today teach AI to read between the lines and sometimes even make jokes? These heroes of code and algorithms are quietly and persistently pushing back the boundaries of the possible, making our future look more and more like an episode of a science fiction series.

Conclusions

While we admire ChatGPT and its amazing skills, let's remember those who laid the groundwork and continue to push the horizons of AI. They may not have become celebrities, but their contributions to the science and technology world are absolutely real. Thanks to them, we can ask AI how to brew coffee properly. And while the AI hasn't learned how to brew it for us yet, who knows what will happen next!

The final bit
GOODBYE TO THE AI (WELL, ALMOST)

And so, dear readers, we have come to the end of our ironic journey through the world of artificial intelligence. If you've reached this point and you haven't turned into a cyborg, congratulations, you're a real hero!

What we've learned (or what we think we've learned)

1. AI won't bite: yes, we've learned that AI is not a sci-fi monster from a Hollywood blockbuster but rather a diligent assistant who sometimes likes to play a prank.

2. From algorithms to miracles: we traced AI's journey from simple algorithms to complex systems capable of amazing things. Remember that behind every miracle are long lines of code and numerous cups of coffee.

3. The future (not so distant): immersed in a world of fantasy and predictions, we realized that the future of AI is full of not only brilliant possibilities but also unpredictable adventures.

Goodbye (but not forever)

As we close this book, the world of AI continues its rapid evolution. Who knows, maybe in the next book of this story, ChatGPT will learn how to make coffee or even pilot a spaceship. Until then, keep your AI handy (or in your smartphone) and remember that the most amazing thing about the future is its unpredictability.

And remember, in a world where AI is constantly learning, it's time for you to start learning along with it. Who knows, maybe the next time you ask ChatGPT something, it will answer not only with information but also with a question that will make you think.

So, until we meet again in the world of AI!

www.ingramcontent.com/pod-product-compliance
Lightning Source LLC
Chambersburg PA
CBHW070145230526
45471CB00002B/518